Get

P.A.I.D.

A Guide to Getting Paid Faster
(and What to Do if You Don't!)

Get P.A.I.D.
A Guide to Getting Paid Faster (and What to Do if You Don't!)

Published by: Business Credit Publications, LLC
Book Design: Droz and Associates

Business Credit Publications, LLC:
2200 Gulf Tower, Pittsburgh, PA 15219

Website: www.getpaidsystem.com

Contents

A New View Of Credit

Chapter 1

Easy credit is often used as a tool to get or keep a customer. Ironically, such policies often have the opposite effect. Using easy credit as a marketing tool can increase marketing costs and reduce margins. In addition, collection procedures for late payments put you and your customer in an adversarial role.

Credit can be best understood as an integral part of a customer relationship that creates parity between what is sold and what is paid for those products and services. The way credit is handled can impact a company's bottom line and can affect the relationship a company has with its vendors and customers.

Understanding the costs of easy credit and ways to avoid it can improve margins, enhance customer relationships and improve the relationship between the sales and credit functions within a company.

A. Four Pillars of Parity

I n the following chapters, we will explore a new way to view credit policy: The Get P.A.I.D. Business System represents an integrated approach to credit policy that views parity with your customer as a fundamental aspect of a healthy buyer/seller relationship. The Get P.A.I.D. System consists of Four Pillars, that together support parity in your relationship with customers.

There are four pillars:
Preparation of policy and procedures
Assessment of credit risk
Implementation of policies
Defense of policies

By employing the Get P.A.I.D. Business System, businesses can make their invoices more than just a bill representing what is owed. An invoice becomes an expression of value delivered to the customer. It is a statement of what has been delivered and a reminder of the understanding between the parties. It is through mutual agreement that parity is achieved.

The Four Pillars of the Get P.A.I.D. Strategy

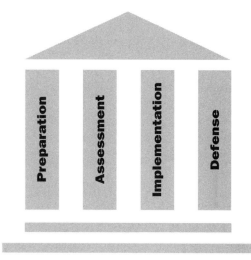

Preparation

What you do before you provide goods or services to develop a clear understanding of the parameters of the transaction and the benefits to the customer for paying promptly or in advance. The key to an effective credit policy is defining and preparing the tools necessary to clarify your policy.

This can involve agreements at the 'front end' and a series of collection procedures at the 'back end' of the process. Having these tools in place can not only help a company define the standards and expectations, with customers and clients but also protect them in the event of slow pay.

Assessment

Establishing tacit or formal agreement with the customer as to the parameters of the relationship. Without an agreement in terms of expectations, customers have every motivation to be lax in their payment habits. The agreement process needs to be an integral part of the sales process to provide customers and clients information about the benefits of advance or early payment, as well as the consequences of late payment.

Implementation

Proactive, tactful engagement with the customer to ensure compliance with the understandings. Specific tools such as invoices, statements and reminders can play an important role in establishing discipline in payment. Discipline is essential in shortening payment cycles. But discipline starts with consistent use of tools and adherence to policy standards.

**Robert's
Rules of Credit**

*Time is of the Essence.
The faster you respond,
the more likely you
will be to collect
what is owned. Don't
assume that a reminder
statement will result
in prompt payment.
Count the days. Letters
should be sent on the
35th and 45th. Call on
the 50th to understand
the circumstances and
get a commitment even
if it's a partial payment.
If the partial is not
received within two
days, call on the 55th.
Proceed with Phase II
tactics on the 61st day.*

Defense

Prompt and proactive response if and when customers do not honor their commitments. If expectations are not met, immediate action is required. With collection tools and processes in place, it becomes a seamless process to define options and responses to a variety of slow pay scenarios.

Interdependence

Although people may be involved (and participate with passion) in intergroup conflict, surprisingly, they are not at fault. Consider the classic labor vs. management struggle. Social scientists have explained that union leaders and managers, no matter how strident or angry, did not cause or create their perpetual conflict. Conflict was designed into their relationship. It is inevitable. If leaders were replaced, many work groups would continue to fight.

Work group conflict and interdependence go hand in hand. Groups like sales and credit depend on each other to complete a transaction and close a deal. Sales' hard-won output—the order—becomes the input for credit. Credit then processes the order and arrives at its own output, the credit terms.

Easy credit approval means a contented sales force, a truce and a sigh of relief. Impose more restrictive terms on a poor credit risk and sales will blame the credit department for cooling customer enthusiasm, jeopardizing the entire transaction and losing a good customer.

The result: seething ill will between interdependent parties.

Companies resolve this built-in conflict in a number of clever ways. The least effective, but all too common solution is to bring the departments together under one supervisor. In our experience, a unified credit/sales department is a recipe for disaster. In this scenario, more credit applications are approved, no matter how risky. Generally, the sales force dominates, while those in credit become frustrated with their inability to insulate the organization against preventable losses.

My father understood this universal problem. He often joked that many sales managers often misquoted Lord Tennyson, saying, "'Tis better to have sold and lost, than never to have sold at all." In other words, the sales side of the business often does its job by selling. *It* doesn't have to worry about collecting for the sale.

Dad recognized the dilemma and never recommended the merger of sales and credit into a single department. What he recommended and what we practice today requires a different understanding of "sales" and "credit" and their relationship.

B. Getting a Grasp on Credit

1. The War Between the Closers

So there's a war going on in your company. It's not about Christine and Mark's epic struggle for the corner office, nor their fight over who really came up with the brilliant idea du jour, nor even the ongoing debate over what kind of coffee should go into the break room machine.

It's a fight to the finish between sales and credit, and its implications are more far-reaching than corner offices or caffeine.

The Sales View

"Conflict and sales just don't mix."

Mark is a salesman. He gets paid to close deals and keep customers happy. And customers, he feels, are happiest when they get what they want. Sometimes this includes liberal credit terms, whether agreed upon in advance or created as the relationship develops. And, although he realizes that it's important for the company to get paid for what he sold, he also feels that discussing the terms of payment, the consequences of late payment and the details of the company's credit policy can be an obstacle to closing a sale. And he knows for sure that collections can be an obstacle to good relationships. After working hard to get an account, he's loath to 'upset' the client with constant battering, collection proceedings and legal action. And Mark's right. War isn't good for sales.

Sales people often use easy credit as a way to keep the customer happy.

9

The Credit View

"Anyone can sell a dollar for 50 cents."

Credit Mangers don't like working for free. They want the bills paid. Now.

Christine is the credit manager. She gets paid to close, as well. She closes the books every month. And it better be with more money taken in than going out. She understands Mark's point of view (even if he *does* refer to her as the "Sales Prevention Department"). But, she believes that anyone can sell a dollar for 50 cents, and having to pay a customer for doing business sounds more like charity than business in her book. There are bills to pay, profits to make and jobs to keep. The customer needs to know that they don't work for free. Christine is right, too. Business is business.

The first casualty? *Efficiency.* Warring groups ignore requests, disrupt the chain of command, sabotage work processes and damage output. And the worst part is that leaders probably don't even smell the gun smoke.

Workplace warfare need not rage openly to cause harm. It can percolate below ground as group distrust, wariness and suspicion. Managers charged with motivating guerilla warriors to cooperate, even minimally, for the good of the organization deserve our sympathy.

2. Credit Policy as a Business Strategy

This is a book about Getting Paid. Getting Paid faster. And collecting those invoices lost in your customer's Neverland, the 'bad debts.'

Unfortunately, by the time you're in collection mode, you've already foregone the opportunity of getting paid fast. You had to have planned for that in advance.
Why does this happen? Five simple words: People don't like paying bills. In a recent survey[1], 43 percent of Americans dislike either paying their bills or balancing their accounts more than any other task.

It doesn't matter if you are rich or poor, it's just something almost everyone despises. For some reason, consumers and businesses alike prefer to hold on to their money as long as possible. There needs to be a good reason for them to pay quickly. The reason that many businesses often don't get paid faster is not accidental. They let it happen by either allowing sales philosophy dictate their credit policy through lack of discipline or not knowing how to create parity between buyer and seller.

Sales and credit are often seen as opposing forces, rather than part of a common goal. This creates parity in the relationship between you and your customer.

Without a system in place that considers all the stages of a credit relationship, collections become a response to inaction on the part of the buyer, as compared to a continuous and proactive policy implemented by the seller to encourage and enforce prompt payment. Getting paid faster is not just a matter of sending collection letters sooner. It is a business strategy that can transform a business to increase profit, enhance the relationship with the customer and reduce overall marketing costs.

C. Sales and Credit

1. Sales Defined

Instead of seeing sales as an organization's engine and credit as its brake, we regard a credit sale as a "loss" to an organization until the bill is paid. It's true that nothing happens in business until something is sold. It's also true that granting our best credit to every customer is like giving every American who said they lived in New Orleans after Hurricane Katrina a $2,000 Federal Emergency Management Association (FEMA) credit card. With giveaway credit and no rules, someone was able to buy lottery tickets or a lavish dinner at Hooters with their windfall, not bread and milk or siding and shingles. And of course, some did.

2. What's Credit?

Credit, too, requires a definition. Wimpy, the overweight sidekick in the Popeye comic strip, had it nailed. The sum total of Wimpy's vocabulary, "I'll gladly pay you Tuesday for a hamburger today," beats any dictionary definition of credit. If Wimpy's hamburger vendor, a 1930s version of McDonald's, was willing to deliver a product today and wait for payment later, he made Wimpy a happy customer, but a debtor. The vendor, of course, became a creditor.

David Sher has another credit example with lots of implications.*

The Story of a Lemonade Stand

"One day last summer, I was jogging in my neighborhood—and it was really hot! I think the temperature was 95 degrees and the humidity was over 100 percent. Toward the end of the run, I was getting very, very thirsty. I glanced ahead and spotted two small boys who appeared to be about seven or eight years old. They were sitting in a front yard with a freshly painted sign that read LEMONADE – 25 CENTS. Man, I was so thirsty I could hardly swallow, but I didn't have any money. So I shuffled over to the boys and asked, 'Excuse me, do you offer credit?' One boy whispered to his friend, 'What's credit?'

I explained that 'credit' is when you buy something now, but you pay for it later. So I asked if I could have the drink now and come back some other time to pay. Even though one of the boys said that would be okay, I wanted to make sure he was comfortable with his decision. So I pointed out the potential problems. I told him that when I came back to pay, he might be gone. What should I do? The boy said to put the money in his mailbox. I told him that I would do that but no one

*The story is from the David Sher book, "Collect Debts"

would be around to watch the mailbox — so someone could come by and take the money.

The bewildered boy looked at his friend and shrugged his shoulders. The other boy hesitated and then turned to him and said, 'Oh, why don't we just give it to him.'

Well, I drank my drink and it was delicious. I walked home and felt guilty. So even though I was tired and could hardly move, I walked back to the lemonade stand. I handed the boy a quarter and a nickel. He looked up at me and asked why I gave him the extra money. I told him that I added some 'interest.' He replied, 'What's interest?'"

Like salesmen everywhere, the boys realized that if they didn't extend credit, they would have fewer customers. They accepted the risk and with very little information about Mr. Sher, sold to him on credit. There seemed to be no division of labor at the lemonade stand. The boys worked together, but neither one was the sales manager or credit manager. Two boys, one combined role. Although the story had a happy ending and it illustrates credit at its most basic level, it also represents our classic recipe for disaster: a scenario where sales, not good sense, dominated.

How should the boys have worked out their problem? The system we advocate and explain further in Chapter 2 requires that every sale, except payment in cash, must pass a company-designed creditworthiness test and be agreed upon with the customer. No one in sales or credit can override or ignore the credit test unless both sales and credit agree on when, where and how that takes place. Further, without a clear understanding between customer and vendor, enforcing a credit policy can become onerous. For the boys, the "Company" might have been a parent, someone with the experience and clout to make and enforce sensible rules.

The Payment Gap

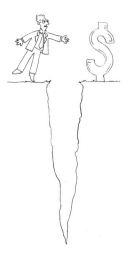

D. The Costs of Credit:

There are good reasons for caution when providing hamburgers, lemonade or any product on credit.

The time between the delivery of a product or service and payment for that deliverable is the crux of a credit policy. The term we use for this time frame is the **Payment Gap**. The smaller the gap, the better the credit. The wider the gap, the longer you wait to get paid. And the wider the chasm between you and your customer.

The reason there are often conflicts between sales and credit departments is that sales people look at easy credit as an advantage to closing sales and keeping customers. It is, in effect, a marketing expense. After all, considering the cost of getting a customer, isn't it worth another 30 or 60 days to keep the customer happy?

Although there are circumstances where this may be true, in far more cases, when the costs are understood, there may be better and more economical ways of enhancing customer relationships. According to this theory, the wider the Payment Gap, the better the relationship with the customer.

But, nothing could be further from reality. As the Payment Gap increases, the costs of collection and maintenance may eventually exceed any benefit that can be derived. This has to do with both the cost of credit and the impact collections have on the customer relationship. Outstanding debt (or outstanding sales) costs money, a lot more than most organizations realize. Payment Gaps create categories of added cost that should be considered:

Finance Cost, the actual cost of financing a customer debt

Opportunity Cost, the cost of giving up access to available capital

Collection Cost, the cost of administration and discounts that are often needed.

Relationship Cost, the cost of losing the good-will of your customer

Marketing Cost, using easy credit as a marketing strategy is a costly form of marketing.

Here are three quick real-world examples. All revolve around Seller's sale of $10,000 worth of product to Buyer.

1. Finance Cost

Basic Finance Cost. Assume that the interest on the money Seller borrowed from the bank to finance its growth and expansion was 1 percent per month. The $10,000 credit Seller extends to Buyer costs it $1,200 per year or, in credit terms, $100 every 30 days. If Buyer takes 90 days to pay its bill, that 90 days costs the Seller $300. For 180 days, a full six months of non-payment, it's a hefty $600.

Sales Margin: Assume that Seller made 6 percent on the $10,000 sale. That's $600. If Buyer did not pay for the product during the normal 30-day grace period, but took an extra 60 days, that extra time cost Seller. How much? With interest at 1 percent per month, the extra 60 days was a $200 expense and reduced Seller's profit margin from $600 to $400.

Stretched payments: What if Buyer stretched out its payment over the next four months? Say it paid $2,000 on time, $2,000 in 30 days, another $2,000 at 60 days, another payment at 90 days and made its final $2,000 payment at 120 days.

With the cost of money at 1 percent per month percent, that arrangement cost Seller $100 every 30 days after Buyer's due date. At the end of those four months, that amounts to a $200 cost to Seller.

It would not take long for Seller to make $0 profit on a $10,000 sale. That's not a healthy prospect for any company. Yet, it happens all the time. And what makes it even more serious is that most businesses don't notice.

2. Opportunity Cost

Of course, there are other costs of a delayed payment. Seller could have found other uses for $300 here and $200 there, such as paying down its own obligations or increasing its inventory. Managers and clerks could have saved time by not worrying about whether Buyer would pay its debts. Opportunity cost, that is, the potential return on investment lost as a result of not having available capital, has been estimated at $1 - 4$ percent per month. Let's say 2 percent per month for opportunity cost.

3. Collection Cost

Reminders by mail or phone also take time, and we all know that time is money. The "reminder" money could have been channeled into more constructive uses, such as servicing the needs of Seller's other customers. And, the longer the credit extension, the greater the cost. After 120 days, the costs of collection can skyrocket as a result of two things: legal fees and accommodations. Often, after repeated reminders, companies turn to two remedies: compromise or legal action. Compromise usually involves substantial reductions in the invoiced amount. Legal costs usually involves a percentage of the collected amount or hourly fees.

Either of these options can trim the collected amounts by as much as 50 percent, in addition to the already-incurred finance and opportunity costs.

4. Relationship Cost

By the time a collection process is required, the probability that a company will keep the customer is low. In this instance, in addition to collection cost is the cost of future revenue and replacement cost, both of which dwarf collection costs. Even if the customer is not lost, there are intangible costs that can erode the relationship like the resentment caused by Buyer's delayed payments. Seller might start neglecting Buyer's needs, ignoring its phone calls and giving preference to other clients. Then Buyer, frustrated over these slights, begins bad-mouthing Seller to others in the marketplace. Another company, getting ready to sign a lucrative contract with Seller, hears these rumors and changes its mind.

We estimate the overall damage to the relationship after 60 days to be 5 percent per month.

You get the picture. Credit costs money. Many companies extend credit without realizing just how *much* it costs.

But one thing's for sure: having a good grasp on what you're risking makes you infinitely more careful about how you play the credit game. Here, as in most areas of life and business, knowledge is power.

5. Cost

When businesses use credit as a marketing tool, to get or keep a customer, there is one last cost: the marketing cost. What percent of the sale is devoted to getting and keeping the customer? Intuition suggests that if a company incurred a 15% expense, to enhance the customer relationship, that 15% might be considered marketing cost. But in reality, the cost is much higher. For example, as shown above, if a company has invoiced $10,000, and incurs a $1,500 expense to collect it, in effect, that's paying $1,500 for an $8,500 dollar sale, or $1,500/$8,500. That's not 15%. That's 17.6%. If the cost, more than 90 days, as shown above, is almost 30% to collect, that's $3,000/$7,000 or almost 43% marketing cost. By the time you get more than 120 days, many companies aren't just losing money on the sale, they're

The Cost of the Payment Gap

actually paying more to keep the customer than the sale was worth in the first place. The chart below lays out these costs and underscores the cost of credit.

Chart 1.1

Cost of $10,000 for Various Payment Gaps						
	Monthly%	30 days	60 days	90 days	120 days	150 days
Finance Cost	1%	$100	$200	$300	$400	$500
Opportunity Cost	2%	$200	$400	$600	$800	$1,000
Collection Cost	1% - 3%	$100	$400	$1,000	$1,500	$3,000
Relationship Cost	5%	0	$500	$1,000	$1,500	$2,000
Total	9% - 39%	$400	$1,500	$2,900	$4,200	$6,500

E. The Red Zone

The Payment Gap brings into focus why uncontrolled credit extension isn't good for bottom line, customer relationships or your marketing budget. Yet, many small businesses toast with champagne when they get a big account. After all, big means they've got money. And of course, they'll pay on time. Right. More often than not, the bigger the company, the better they understand benefits of the Payment Gap... for them.

There are a lot of reasons that customers want to extend the Payment Gap. Some don't have the money, possibly because their own credit policy has some problems. Sometimes there is a justifiable problem with the product or service they received and customers withhold payment until the issue is resolved. Some are just mooches who delight in the passive-aggressive pleasure of withholding your hard-but-yet-unearned compensation.

For many companies, however, having vendors finance their businesses is simply a matter of policy. They know the value of a 60- or 90-day Payment Gap to their bottom line and so long as a vendor will go along, why wouldn't they take it?

Better management of credit for your own benefit comes first by understanding the costs of different Payment Gaps, the benefits of early payment and most importantly, the reasons why customers choose to pay **ahead** of delivery, **on** delivery or 150 days **past** delivery of a product or service. Because of the cost of extended credit, the Payment Gap is one of the most valuable manageable assets of a company and can be the determining factor in managing cash flow, costs and customer satisfaction.

Just as extending credit can be costly, advance or on-delivery payments have the opposite effect: They can actually enable your customer to finance your business. By asking for an advance, you are in effect getting an interest-free loan. It also "invests" the customer earlier in the sale.

On the other hand, by letting the Payment Gap extend more than 60 days, it becomes a danger zone: the "Red Zone" of the Payment Gap. It increases collection cost, often results in accommodations to settle the account and can compromise the relationship with your customer.

The chart below represents the value and/or cost of extending the payment gap and indicates the Payment Gap "Red Zone," where the costs begin to skyrocket.

Payment Gap Costs

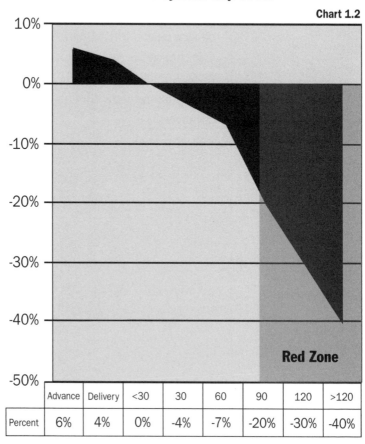

Chart 1.2

	Advance	Delivery	<30	30	60	90	120	>120
Percent	6%	4%	0%	-4%	-7%	-20%	-30%	-40%

F. Evaluating Your Customer

You can tell a lot about a country's priorities by looking at what it reads. And Americans like to read about selling stuff. Despite its great potential for harm, credit comes in a distant second to sales in America's book preferences. We used the Web site, ABEbooks.com as a measure of the popularity of books that have either "sales," "credit" or "debt" in the title. ABEbooks.com claims to have 100 million new, used or out-of-print books available from more than 13,000 booksellers. Searching for titles that mentioned either "sales" or "sale" yielded 63,806 books, including *Secrets of Closing Sales* and *Earning What You're Worth?: The Psychology of Sales Call Reluctance*. Multiple copies of the same book were included in that vast sales library. Popular fiction also surfaced. "Credit" was about a third as popular with 19,301 books, including some personal finance texts on money management and home loans. "Debt" was central to 20,588 books with a few fictional titles like a Tom Clancy novel (*Debt of Honor*) and a Harlequin romance (*Debt of Dishonor*) mixed in.

What this little exercise tells me is that selling is hot. We like to read about it. We want to do it better. Credit . . . well, maybe we consider it a little dull. But we surely aren't bored by *getting paid* and, as the title of this book attests, that's what lurks at the heart of this subject.

Correcting the imbalance between America's preference for sales over credit is one of the goals of this book. We have already looked at the possibility that the poor relationship between sales and credit is due to task interdependence, not personality differences. Fix the interdependency and we have alleviated a large area of conflict.

G. Evaluating Your Policy – Causes of Bad Debt

Further improvement in the sales-credit relationship can be accomplished by digging into the root causes of extending the Payment Gap. Many, but certainly not all Payment Gaps are created by the companies that extend the credit. That's right. If we didn't extend credit to people or companies who can't handle it or extend it without considering the costs, those people or companies wouldn't become delinquent. That's good news.

It's always better to change our own behavior than to try to change others.

Our experience points to four internal causes of entering the Red Zone.

1. Unsupportive Culture: The mother of all credit problems is a culture that assumes slow or no pays are inevitable and a necessary business evil. Cultures that condone, excuse or expect bad debt soon have their prophecies fulfilled.

Isolating cultural issues and correcting them is tricky. Those involved in isolating and correcting are also usually immersed in the culture, knee-deep in the swamp they are trying to drain. Outside consultants, seminars by credit professionals or even lunch with colleagues point out cultural issues, like the missing car keys, are often hidden in plain sight.

Novice credit workers, full of innocence and enthusiasm, often drain the swamp for us. A new employee for one of our clients tackled accounts that were judged impossible to collect, the deadbeat files, the professional no pays, at least according to her boss and the prevailing culture. Not knowing that the task

was impossible, she begged, pleaded, sold, cajoled, investigated and… collected a lot of money.

2. Bad Management: Experiences, such as joining a civic club, going on a first date or paying a bill on time, often begin with a request. Managers who are afraid to ask for the money, who fear offending customers or who encourage timidity among staff members set the wrong tone for their department. Instead of developing ways to get paid promptly, they inspire complexity, confusion, indecision, cumbersome reports, minimal delegation and a willingness to allow reduced payments.

In our practice, we've seen clients with bad management. Back in the day, we took on a number of collection accounts for a lumber supply company.

As part of the document package, we received copies of the "account card" showing the customer's purchase and payment activity. Each card had a credit limit set and clearly recorded at the top, but in almost every case, the balance due was significantly higher than the credit limit! When I asked the client how that happened, he told me that they had no system in place for the sales clerks to check the credit limit when making a sale. How is that for mixed messages to the sales team!

Actions always speak louder than policies. One client had very clear documents that specified payment terms and deadlines for its customers. The trouble was that they rarely called or pressed until the customer was 60 days past due. Even then, they would almost always waive the late charges and interest. The client's actions in allowing the 60-day extension clearly told the customers they could always plan on paying late.

3. Lack of Policy: A company's mission statement outlines its purpose, vision and what it wants to accomplish. One step down are general principles of action and behavior such as "We will endeavor to collect 90 percent of all accounts within 90 days," or "We will diversify our customer base." Policies go deeper. They are the specifics—the rules to live by. They answer the critical day-to-day question *Who does what, when, where and how?* Policies that are unwritten are unstable, lax and unclear. They give new customers the impression that it's OK to be late, that there are no consequences for missing a payment or two. There will be more on policies in Chapter 2.

4. Lack of People Skills: We're all human beings. Yes, including that evasive, phone-call dodging customer who owes you $20,000. Like all humans, even diehard debtors respond more openly to people who want to build a relationship with them and treat them with respect. In other words, those who approach debtors feeling self-righteousness or timid and apologetic usually find a closed door.

Credit workers who show interest, listen attentively, empathize and still enforce the rules should train the rest of the staff. They will always get further and bring in more money than those who focus on rule enforcement alone.

Anyone who has been in an argument knows that some words are "right" while others should be avoided. My father taught me to say "I want" in a family argument and not "You did." In our practice, we've discovered that "initialing an agreement" is less threatening than "signing a contract." Think about it. For ages, mothers have cautioned their sons and daughters not to "sign" anything lawyers or military recruiters put in front of them. Few warn against "initialing" or "okaying."

Similarly, "investment" or "invest" creates a sense of pride of ownership in a product purchased on credit. "Payment" or "pay" connotes inferiority or settling a score. By asking a debtor to "make a remittance on their investment with a check," people-savvy employees get paid with a smile.

Here is an example of a smart way to speak to a slow paying account: "On a scale of one to 10, where are you with respect to getting this matter resolved?" For debtors who continually give the matter a low rating, go a step further: "Obviously this is not going to be resolved without resorting to litigation." Saying it this way hints at a legal solution and skillfully avoids the often toothless phrase we've ignored since childhood: "We'll sue."

No matter how difficult the conversation, smart credit departments value persistence, non-emotional words, humor, tactful questioning and conversation enhancing phrases like, "Uh huh," "I see," and "Go on." There will be more on this topic in Chapter 4.

H. Forces Beyond Your Control

In fashioning a supportive credit culture and wise credit policies, it is good to remember that credit, like reputation, extends beyond the walls and into the larger community. Credit issues are no longer an internal matter. State and federal laws regulate the treatment of debtors and those whose businesses fail. There are limits to what we can say and do concerning debtors.

Attorneys know firsthand that going to court to settle a credit dispute is expensive, time consuming and frustrating. It is an experience to be avoided and although our firm handles creditors' rights cases, my goal is to champion prevention and keep credit disputes out of court.

Congratulations . . . you've taken the first step on the GET P.A.I.D. journey. Now that you've expanded your understanding of credit—and discovered why its evil offspring, bad debt, is such a problem for companies— it's time to get specific. In the next chapter, we will lay out the four-step process for writing good credit rules.

Preparation

The first step in a strong Get P.A.I.D. strategy, is Preparation. There must be a system in place that facilitates payment. You must have a credit policy. And not just any credit policy — you likely already have that — but one that's well thought out, thorough, and easily understood by employees in every department in your company.

Writing a credit policy that works for you (instead of, as is too often the case, against you) is a task that should not be taken lightly. You know you should seek guidance from a credit expert (Yep, that's us!) to ensure that your i's are dotted and t's are crossed. What you may not know is that representatives from both sides of the fence—sales and credit—should have a hand in crafting this document. And everyone in your company should have at least a passing acquaintanceship with the final product.

Remember, your ultimate goal is to create a credit conscious culture. Take the time to craft an airtight, yet customer friendly credit policy that makes sense with the rest of your operations as well as your reputation and brand.

A. Establishing Rules

Understanding credit as a business strategy can help you see your credit policy in a new light. Adventure loving, can-do Americans revere the notion that "Rules are made to be broken." It's practically in our DNA that guidelines, commandments, laws, regulations and policies are just too rigid to be taken seriously.

Some credit managers value another old adage: "The best rules are those that are unwritten." That twist makes credit policy flexible and customer friendly. Or, said another way, inconsistent and arbitrary. The truth is, credit policies created on the fly may keep some customers happy, but they do little to encourage long-term business survival.

Here's another problem: cobweb-strewn, moth-eaten credit policies. Some credit policies that find their way into policy manuals live in perpetuity. If they are not updated or revised, they can lose their relevance or effectiveness in a very short time. Employees charged with enforcing these timeworn restrictions usually ignore them.

Despite their seeming lack of popularity, credit rules — especially those that are periodically reviewed and updated — do have an upside. A very big, potentially profitable upside, in fact. Successful entrepreneurs who recognize that credit policy needs to be integrated into their business strategy, know that credit rules have three laudable, strategic goals:

- They force a customer to make a commitment to the transaction.
- They protect the company bottom line.
- They spread credit consciousness throughout the organization.

B. Four Steps To Preparation

Preparing a good credit policy involves four steps:

Step I: Anticipation

1. Six Magic Words

One of the first things you learn as a salesperson is that every prospect has six magic words that can crash a sale. "I'd like to think about it." It's called the "buyer's prerogative," and if you haven't dealt with those six words early in the presentation, you simply haven't anticipated what actually happens in about 90% of sales presentations. Chances are, by the time those words are uttered, you're stuck and probably going home without an order. The prospect just shut you down by making you feel better than you would have felt if the prospect would have said "I'm not interested."

If you're successful closing the sale, the customer has six more words up his sleeve. We've all heard the line, "The check is in the mail" and the disingenuous nature of the statement. The implication is that people say the darnedest things to make you feel good. Unfortunately, by the time those words are uttered, the check is already late and it's not really in the mail.

Robert's Rules of Credit

Contrary to common belief, pre-sale paperwork does not kill a sale. Like many delicate situations in life, presentation is everything. Add consideration and respect to a legal-size credit application and customers are more likely to sign it.

By preparing, you can anticipate and prevent Payment Gaps.

Yet, despite the eventuality of Payment Gaps, we often don't take specific steps to secure the best possible terms for you and your customer. By preparing, you can anticipate and prevent Payment Gaps.

2. Are You Sure You Want To Do This?

Our first step begins with a gut-wrenching question: "Are we willing to take the time to think through this threat and develop ways of protecting our vital interests?" The answer has to be "Yes," but we shouldn't rush the decision. Let the emotional implications, pressure-filled confrontations and consequences of denying credit sink in. Written policies solve problems, but since they involve deciding to do "A," but not "B," they create a few problems of their own.

Part of the reason credit policies remain unwritten is that the majority of customers pay their bills promptly and are good credit risks. Instead of being a threat, these debtors are the lifeblood of an organization. Written policies should not harm or anger prompt payers, but the thought of losing them is enough to weaken the resolve of even the most focused policy writer.

3. Red Zone Debtors

The real threat to business comes from three kinds of problem debtors. These are the debtors that take you into the Red Zone and can cost you big time.

- **Slow Payers:** These debtors promise, stall, even threaten and lie, but they eventually pay their bills. Some fall behind because of other "more pressing" obligations; others are as careless about their bills as they are about other business and family responsibilities. Some regard a bill as a nuisance that they'll take care of on their schedule, not the creditor's. The most difficult members of this group need the threat of litigation or a lien to pay up. They pay their debts only when dire consequences outweigh the benefits of delaying payment.

- **Bi-Polar Debtors:** Some debtors are model citizens in the community and deadbeats to their creditors. It may come as a surprise to say, the museum director, that one of his leading benefactors is a chronic no pay. These individuals save face by selectively rewarding some contacts — the United Way, the arts, local charities — while ignoring their business debts. The most difficult members of this group threaten creditors with harassment lawsuits and fabricate disputes. They are pillars of the community who have a perpetual beef with their creditors. Strong policies can dislodge the bi-polar debtor, but resolution of these disputes is not easy or pretty.

- **Credit Criminals:** These are smart, but pathological, debtors. They enter into agreements with no intention of paying. They are covered by shell corporations with elaborate protections that allow them to liquidate assets and pocket the cash. Their final insult is to skip town with no forwarding address.

Surgically precise polices make life difficult or uncomfortable for credit criminals, bi-polar debtors and slow payers while pampering those who pay on-time. These policies benefit on-time payers by making it clear what they have to do to BE on-time payers and keep their credit "clean." The policies also benefit those with good credit because they make it easy to get credit decisions made when a good credit risk needs a credit line. Further, customers who pay on time want to do business with you and understand that you're important. There's parity in the relationship.

At this early stage, some executives make two preparation decisions—one to undertake policy deliberation and the other to justify their actions. Those who add this second decision find it convenient to blame the corporate lawyer, banker or accountant for policy change. These traditional rule-making professions have taken the heat before and customers understand, and some even accept, their dictates as facts of business life. The truth is, change goes down easier when there's someone in authority to blame. (As a lawyer, I know this facet of human nature all too well!)

Streamlining, growth, mergers and expansion are other frequently cited reasons for saying, "We apologize for the inconvenience, but our policies have changed."

Step II. The Get P.A.I.D. Toolbox

Every tool in a credit manager's toolbox is designed to protect the organization. Like an insurance policy or burglar alarm, it puts something in place now so we'll have fewer regrets later.

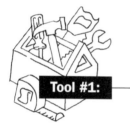

Tool #1:

Advance deposits: This is like asking Wimpy for 25 cents today as a down payment for his $1 hamburger. Such a policy nicely satisfies all three policy goals. It insures customer buy-in, protects the bottom line and gives proof internally and externally that the company is serious about collecting its debts.

Tool #2:

Final payment upon receipt: Wimpy's hamburger vendor could not implement this sensible policy. He already gave Wimpy the hamburger on pure credit or with a 25-cent deposit. Final payment came on Tuesday long after the hamburger had been delivered, consumed and digested. This policy works only when there is some lag time between initial order and later delivery.

It's ok to decline to extend credit! Make sure you do it for the right reasons and comply with any statutes or regulations. This may be the best way to prevent a loss for the right (or "wrong") customer.

That interval allows a debtor to obtain the funds and complete the transaction.

Final payment upon receipt coupled with an advance deposit is an efficient policy, but one rarely seen outside of small business.

Today vendors are much more willing than they were even five years ago to shift their credit risk to a credit card company. A modern vendor would be happy to give Wimpy a hamburger today if he paid with a credit card today. In this arrangement, everyone is doing what they do best: vendors are selling, customers are buying, and the credit card company is assuming the risk (and getting paid to do it.)

Contributing to the decline of final payment on receipt is a lack of trust in those who sell us what we need. Customers want to examine merchandise after delivery and before final payment. Because this simple, effective policy doesn't always apply, we now have an array of more sophisticated, if burdensome tools.

Tool #3:

Payment due in 30 days: Such a policy gives the customer time to examine the merchandise before payment comes due. While this policy defines credit extension for thousands of businesses, it places an administrative burden on creditors. Someone has to calculate the due date, keep track of the time interval, and call to inquire if the payment is late.

Tool #4:

Late fees: With this sensible policy the credit department helps recoup some of the company's credit costs. Late fees also rescue profit from the clutches of slow payers and send a clear message to employees that this is a credit conscious culture. "We're serious about collecting late fees" is a marvelous shared ethic. Putting that slogan on company tee shirts or buttons may convince even the kindest soul that this policy is an expectation of the credit department. *(NOTE: Don't have the sales team wear these shirts!)*

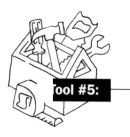

Tool #5:

The Credit Application: A well-constructed credit application is a credit manager's secret weapon. It may not leap tall buildings in a single bound, but it can make the difference between recovery and write-off. This instrument combines basic business-related information with important credit terms and then asks for a signature so that the information can be verified and relied upon.

Desktop publishing has made producing custom-made credit application forms easy and practical. Avoid over-the-counter, all–purpose credit applications; custom is better.

For commercial credit applications I recommend collecting *all of the following* information. Each item is important either for deciding a customer's credit worthiness or in tracking down credit criminals.

- Legal business name

- Primary contact person (not a department)

- Name of owner or CEO (the person you might have to track down in the event of problems)

- Names of officers and directors

- Mailing address

- Previous mailing addresses for business with this name

- Type of business: (Manufacturer, Distributor, Reseller, End User, Service)

- Business structure: (Sole Proprietor, Partnership, Corporation, Limited Liability Company)

- Years in business under this name

- Primary contact person's phone number with extension

- Primary contact person's fax number

- E-mail for primary contact person

- Company Web site

- Federal identification number or owner/ CEO's Social Security number

- Name and address of bank with account numbers

- Three trade references (the customer's vendors)

- Requested credit limit

- Signature of authorized buyer

- Witness. Although there is usually no need for a witness, be careful that the person signing the application is also authorized to make purchases. If the account becomes delinquent, this is who you may face in court.

Tool #6:

The Credit Agreement

This document provides the terms and conditions of a credit relationship and sets the ground rules for any future conflicts. It is one of the credit manager's sharpest tools. It is especially useful for new, large or risk-prone accounts.

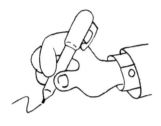

Credit agreements may be printed on the reverse of a credit application or as a second sheet. I find it more convenient to have the application on one side and the terms on the back. The customer need only sign once on the front of the document—the fewer signatures the better. They then review — or skim — the back page where all the heavy artillery and legalese are located.

A credit agreement's airtight language and dogged approach to protecting the creditor's rights makes it one of the best defenses against credit criminals. Here are the provisions I recommend for a business customer:

- **Waiver of jury trial**
  Credit criminals find wiggle room in asking for a lengthy and costly jury trial. This provision waives a jury trial in the honeymoon phase of a relationship.

- **Choice of law provision**
  Sellers—or their attorneys—usually understand the laws in their state (or know which states are favorable) and want them to apply in any dispute.

- **Jurisdiction**
  This provision, also known as forum selection, partners with "choice of law." Usually a creditor wants disputes resolved close to home—their home, not the debtor's. Ordinary legal boilerplate

may not be strong enough here. Make sure that it is impossible for a credit criminal to challenge whose jurisdiction applies.

- **Payment terms**
  Here are the due dates, rates, discounts, late fees, percentages and payment options—the heart of a good, working credit relationship.

- **Interest**
  When are late fees assessed? At what percentage rate? Unless creditors obtain a signature on an agreement to pay a late fee, they may not be able to legally collect one.

- **Attorney fees**
  A creditor who wins in court is often not allowed to recover reasonable attorney fees from the debtor unless the contract clearly requires it. Be careful that the wording is broad enough to meet the variety of state laws that protect debtors in court.

- **Limit of liability**

  If a defective part sold by Company A is installed in a machine owned by Company B and causes the machine to break down, then workers are idled, costly repairs undertaken and profits suffer. By limiting liability, the most Company B would receive as a result of Company A's defective part is a refund.

- **Alternative Dispute Resolution**

  The old saying, "Plan for the best, expect the worst," applies to alternative dispute resolution (ADR). It forewarns debtors that if the normal collection process fails, the creditor wants to try one last face-to-face attempt to get paid before turning the account over to an attorney or collection professional. There are two typical forms of ADR mediation and arbitration. All that is needed in the credit agreement is a statement that alternative dispute resolution will be employed in the case of non-payment. There will be more about ADR in chapter 6.

Tool #7:

- **No modification**

  All informal modifications to the agreement—a waiver of interest one month or an extended payment date six months later—are invalidated. Only written modifications signed by the creditor and debtor change the account agreement.

Credit Enhancements These documents provide leverage and protection, especially for new, untested accounts. They improve the quality of the credit from the creditor's perspective.

- **Personal guarantee**

  The president or owner agrees to pay the bill from personal funds if the agreement is breached. I like the personal guarantee because it tests the business owner's motivation and determination. Before my father went to law school, he needed a $50,000 loan to expand his business. During the loan discussion, the banker asked him if Marlene (my mother) was willing to guarantee the loan. Dad said he would check with her. That evening, he asked and she agreed. When it came time to complete the loan documents, there was no document for my mother to sign.

When my father questioned the omission, the banker said, "I just wanted to know if she was willing to risk her security, her world, for you. If she lacked confidence in you, that would tell me a lot."

Like other tools in the credit agreement, this one may not be universally applicable. It is doubtful that Michael Dell signs personal guarantee agreements for typical purchases by Dell Computers. However, for smaller companies controlled by someone in the business that needs credit, it is ideal.

- **Lien against merchandise**
  The creditor keeps a string (UCC lien) on the merchandise until it is paid for. Although usually sensible, this provision might not always apply. We once represented a company that sold explosives to the coal mining industry. Once the merchandise was delivered and used, there was nothing left for a lien. When merchandise sticks around longer than dynamite, it may be worth discussing this reasonable enhancement.

- **Purchase money security interest**

  When a new customer wants a large order, a creditor might agree only if the customer signs a purchase money security interest (PMSI). A PMSI is similar to the lien on merchandise, only more specific. Tell potential debtors up front that this credit enhancer may be necessary. See chapter 5 for more on the advantages of a PMSI.

- **Letter of credit**

  The debtor's bank sets aside part of the debtor's credit line to pay a creditor's claim on default. There will be more about letters of credit in chapter 5.

- **Letter of confirmation**

  This is one of those "nice things to do" that has a profound effect on judges. A letter of confirmation restates the transaction—amount, time of delivery, price, terms of credit—then adds, "If this does not reflect your understanding, please contact me."

Step III: Using The Tools

The "Who, What, When, Where and How" of Tool Use

Now that the toolbox is put together, under what circumstances do we start using the tools? Which wrench or screwdriver is selected first? Who uses it? These critical policy decisions are not easy to formulate and many companies ignore or defer them. Companies that get paid think them through. Here are a few of the questions every company needs to ask along with our suggested answers:

1. Who is responsible for completing the credit application?

Applications are usually completed on paper or online by the customer. That's the person with the authority to make purchases and sign documents. Since the signature is an agreement to credit terms, be sure the person signing it can live by the terms.

2. How is the credit application verified?

If a credit request or order amount is minimal, the verifier is often someone skilled at applying the "sniff test." They decide if the application smells good, makes sense and looks OK. For larger orders, someone designated by the credit department should call trade and banking references, obtain credit bureau reports, or contact a credit reporting firm (like Dun and Bradstreet or NACM).

In certain industries, like wholesale electrical suppliers or mining equipment suppliers, where there are a few close-knit vendors, it is a good idea to call someone from that exclusive pool for information on a new customer. That's what friends are for.

3. Who is responsible for explaining credit terms to the customer in advance of delivery?

Ideally, this would be the person in sales or credit who obtained the customer's signature. But most often no one has this responsibility. Since credit terms are clearly outlined on the application, sellers don't want to draw attention to them or open them for negotiation.

Customers either accept the terms or walk away. But this "take it or leave it" approach needs to be tempered for customers with large accounts, complex schedules and customized installations. Large accounts need customer service. Consider appointing someone with the authority to explain credit terms to your largest and most important customers and provide them with some credit wiggle room.

4. How are credit limits set?

Begin by repeating this mantra: "Certain kinds of customers are entitled to certain defined credit limits." For new businesses with no credit history, limits should be conservative. After six months of on-time payments, consider a policy that raises the limits by an agreed upon percentage, say 25 percent. For customers that have been in business for five years or more with no delinquencies, their limits may be even more generous. With one or more delinquencies, the limits may be less generous. At the other extreme, for large accounts, credit limits may be part of the negotiation process. For example, credit limits for a customer buying a large inventory may change depending on the amount of down payment and change again as the delivery progresses.

Once credit limit policies are determined, they should be enforced – a prospect some find more distasteful than creating the policy. If you cringe at the thought of enforcement, keep this truth in mind: good customers like clear, fair, reasonable rules better than no rules at all.

5. What happens when a customer misses a payment?

My recommendation is to wait five days after a payment is due. Then call the customer, say that you have not received payment and add, "I just wanted to be sure everything was okay." Many times the late payment results from a paperwork error or a misdirected invoice. If a high percentage of customers, say 80 percent, are late on Day 5, but pay by Day 10 and you can identify who they are, then concentrate scarce resources on calling the other 20 percent. Maybe the policy evolves into "Call all late accounts on Day 15." If you find that customers called on Day 15 are paying by Day 20, consider changing the policy to calling all late accounts on Day 10.

Having a call policy is far better than making it up as you go along. Use your experience to modify customer behavior. As you formulate a late payment policy, keep in mind that some people pay only when asked.

6. Do we insist on a late fee?

The school solution to this question is "Yes," but it is a good idea to air the issue with the collection staff. Debtors always request late fee reductions and because "it's only company policy," someone in collections may be willing to go along. But that ethic has to be nurtured with reminders, rewards and praise. Pure accident may cause an otherwise valuable customer to miss a payment. The policy should provide some latitude for waiver of these late charges as an accommodation. Otherwise a customer who has had a perfect payment record for five years and happens to be one day late with payment, may very well be angered.

7. What do you do when you're unable to collect the balance?

This is the question every company needs to answer. Here is a typical plan: A reminder letter when the account is 15 days delinquent, another at 30 days, a phone call at 45 days, a letter and phone call at 60 days. If there is no payment by then, consider raising the bar and referring the debtor to the company collection department, a collection agency or a law firm that will remind the

debtor of the various credit agreement provisions. The worst plan is to make it up as you go along or hope that things will somehow improve.

Companies that balk at relying on a collection agency or law firm and getting less than the full amount they are owed might remember how clothing stores handle excess inventory. At the end of the season, they discount their merchandise, put it on sale and get rid of it. Like today's fashions, delinquent accounts rarely get better with age.

8. What incentives will we offer for prompt payment?

Some debtors take advantage of every discount they are offered. They pay in 10 days in order to earn a 2 percent early-pay discount. This frugality results in a sizable savings. On a $100,000 purchase, for example, a 2 percent discount saves the customer $2,000. On the other side, a 20-day acceleration on a 30-day credit can save the seller about $450 (at an 8 percent annual borrowing rate).

9. Who is responsible for giving customers permission to reduce their payments?

Carefully consider who has this authority and flexibility. The best candidate is someone who is a superb and adaptable negotiator with excellent people and accounting skills. He or she has to juggle business costs associated with each creative payment scheme — 25 percent a week for the next four weeks or split the payments over the next two months — and adapt the scheme to the customer. Equally important is who should not handle this delicate responsibility.

Depending on its collection philosophy, a company may want an enforcer, not a negotiator in this role — someone who politely, but forcibly, insists on the terms in the agreement.

Step IV: Review and Refine The Toolkit

The vital components of every machine wear out and need replacing. Metals, people, and policies experience "fatigue" and, over time, break under pressure. At least every two years discuss and review the company's credit weapons and policies. What needs to be fixed, replaced or abandoned?

We have found that this review is best accomplished in an organized fashion by a team consisting of representatives of the company's sales, credit extension and collection staff, along with outside collection professionals. Getting these folks together will allow a full review of how the current policies are working and how they aren't.

Got all that? Good! You're well on your way to implementing and perfecting a system that will allow you to apply the GET P.A.I.D. business strategy more regularly and with far less hassle than you've ever experienced.

Assessment Of Risk

Obviously, you can't GET P.A.I.D. unless you extend credit only — or at least primarily — to customers who are likely to pay. And therein lies the crux of the creditor's dilemma. Who is likely to pay? Who isn't? And how can you make sure you loan your money to the former and politely send the latter on their merry way?

The simple answer is: do your homework. This chapter explains how to conduct a thorough investigation of the three Cs: Character, Capacity and Capital. It also covers guidelines for negotiating terms, improving (if not overhauling) your billing practices, and figuring out when to clamp down on customers who've proven unworthy of your generous credit limits.

A. The Importance of Assessment

Credit application? *Check.*
Credit agreement? *Check.*
Credit enhancements? *Check.*
Policies? *Check.*

So, you're prepared.

The next step in the Get P.A.I.D. System is assessing the credit and defining the proper precautions to integrate the credit information with your credit policy. This process begins by reviewing the credit applications to separate the applications of honest customers from those of credit criminals—a task that may appear to be routine and easy, but should never be taken lightly.

At a minimum, all applications must pass a good, healthy "sniff test." Admittedly, that's not a scientific term but we're talking intuition here, which is more art than science. But remember, the sniff test—determining whether something "looks OK" or "makes sense"— is only the beginning. The material in this chapter goes beyond sniffing, intuition and first impressions. You should do a lot of detective work before arriving at a credit decision.

B. The Three Cs of Credit

The sleuthing we recommend revolves around the three "Cs" of credit: the *Character* of the borrower/customer, the *Capacity* of the customer to shoulder additional debt and the amount of *Capital* the customer needs to maintain a favorable asset-to-liability ratio. Two of the "Cs" are easier to research; the third can only be approximated by outsiders. To assess the "Three Cs," we recommend:

1. Checking the white and yellow pages of the telephone directory. Does the listed address and phone number agree with what's on the credit application? This is actually better than an online directory. Many companies still feel that a real "phone book" listing is a marketing essential and will take care to see that the information is up to date.

2. Calling directory assistance (411) or searching online for the company's phone number. Is it the same as the one on the application?

3. Do a "Google" or other online search. What do you learn about the company and the owners? Follow the trail.

4. Calling bank references. Local bankers may require a copy of the signed credit application with authorization to release information before answering any account questions on the phone or in writing. Typical deposit-related questions are:

- When was the account opened?
- Where does the company maintain its office? What address do you have for this account?
- Is there any overdraft or not sufficient funds (NSF) activity?
- What is the current balance in their checking account? In their savings account? (Some bankers prefer to quote a balance range, not an exact figure.)
- Is the client in good standing?

When the customer has a loan relationship with the bank, these questions may be added:

- What type of loan does the client have with you?
- When was the loan opened?
- What is the account balance (or balance range)?
- Has the client paid as agreed?

Consider going one step further and inquiring about the character of the company:

- What can you tell me about the owner/ president?
- Is she or he involved in the community?
- Is she or he a member of any local organizations or civic groups?
- What is your impression of him/her?
- Do you know anyone else who can vouch for his or her character? Follow up with these secondary references.

As in all such inquiries, it is better to speak personally with the banker and sidestep formal written answers. Non-contextual cues—tone, inflection, hesitations, even contradictions—may reveal more than numbers and words on a form. Indeed, it may be that the banker wants to tell you something without actually "telling" you, so give him or her the opportunity to do so.

5. Calling business or trade references.

These organizations already have a credit relationship with your potential customer. Profit from their experience by asking:

- When was the account opened?
- What is their credit limit?
- Do they pay on time?
- Average days late?
- What is the date of your last sale to them?
- What is the amount owed?
- What is the age of their account?

Let's assume the company gave you two other trade references. *When calling, ask this follow-up question:* "Do you know of businesses other than those two that have a credit relationship with the company?" If other names are provided, call them and ask the same questions.

Although the employment law litigation boom has made some people fearful of giving employment references, some businesses still follow the Golden Rule in credit-related interactions. They want to be helpful so that others will be honest with them when the situation is reversed.

6. Getting a credit bureau report.

This is a good way to obtain certain basic information about a prospective client, but don't put undue reliance on it. Credit criminals have mastered techniques for fabricating and falsifying credit information. They are successful because credit-reporting agencies often fail to verify or update information before publishing their reports. Use credit reports from Dun & Bradstreet, National Association of Credit Management (NACM), Experian, TransUnion or Equifax to double-check information already obtained from credit applications and other references. Where these reports really justify their cost is in their ability to report negative information: small claims judgments, tax liens and bankruptcies. Few credit applicants volunteer this information.

Visit their Web sites to compare products, services and fees:

www.dnb.com/us, 1-800-234-3867

www.peacm.com, 1-800-559-6226
(an NACM affiliate)

www.experian.com, 1-888-397-3742

www.transunion.com, 1-800-888-4213

www.equifax.com, 1-800-685-1111

For business reports, we prefer Dun & Bradstreet or NACM.

7. Checking with your credit association or industry group.

Make use of professional contacts in the credit field. Credit associations like NACM offer educational, networking and support opportunities to their members in communities across the country. It is highly likely that at least one NACM member in your area already knows your potential customer. Benefit from their experience. Visit the NACM Web site, **www.nacm.org** to see what they offer.

8. Calling competitors.

If you have a cordial or friendly relationship with competitors, check to see if they were the customer's previous vendor. If yes, ask them the same questions you would any other business or trade reference. In addition, ask *why* the company is no longer a customer. Remember, if the customer was buying from someone else and now wants to "bestow" its business on you, unless you have a significant price, service or quality advantage, you should wonder why this "gift" is arriving now. Credit issues, perhaps?

9. Obtaining a current financial statement.

For new customers with significant credit needs, request a recent financial statement. This could be one prepared internally, by outside accountants or completed on a form you provide. Especially check their debt-to-equity ratio. Generally a ratio of .5 to 1.5 is acceptable.

C. Credit Limits, Discounts, Late Fees

With all the information at hand, it is time to merge data with policy. According to your company's application policy, did the potential credit customer pass review? If character and capacity information are vague or confusing, do more checking. In some cases, where the information "smells" fraudulent, consider calling in the pros: local or state law enforcement agencies. Many of them will be familiar with fraud-by-credit (or "bust out") schemes where criminals then disappear with the goods.

Some companies prefer to bypass detective work altogether. Their policy is to do a cursory review, grant a small credit line and review their decision after six months of customer experience. Others take the opposite approach. They want to know everything they can possibly find out about their customer. Their credit decisions hinge on the in-depth investigation we recommend. In either case, the credit pot can be sweetened with negotiations regarding credit limits, discounts and late fee exceptions.

Here are some of the more typical arrangements:

1. Limits: Two 10 percent rules coexist. One states that the upper limit on credit should be no higher than 10 percent of the customer's net worth. When a customer is a large business, that rule can create an uncomfortably high ceiling. The other rule tempers the first: no one customer should account for more than 10 percent of the credit-granting company's annual business. Do the math for your business and then use your best judgment, keeping in mind that new businesses can easily obtain $50,000 credit limits from some credit card issuers.

2. Discounts and payment terms: Discounts rarely exceed three percent, but they are an excellent means of encouraging prompt payment from honest, conscientious debtors. "Payment terms" refer to when and how the invoice is to be paid. Typically there are two time periods. One is attached to the discount and is usually between 10 and 15 days. If the bill is paid within that period, the customer is permitted to take a discount, often two percent. If the discount period is ignored, the other time period applies and the

Get P.A.I.D.

A Guide to Getting Paid Faster (and What To Do If You Don't!)

full amount of the invoice is due, typically in 30 days. In Accounting 101, that equation is written as 2/10 net 30. A buyer who takes a 2 percent discount on a $1,000 purchase ($1,000 x .02 = $20) pays $980 if the check arrives within the 10-day window, otherwise she pays the entire $1,000 by Day 30.

Discounts and terms vary from industry to industry. Perishable goods often require terms shorter than 30 days. Discounts and terms for meat, dairy products and vegetables are typically 1/7 net 10 and 2/10 net 11. Longer terms, sometimes up to 180 days, are normal in manufacturing. In European and Asian countries, our generally accepted net 30 becomes their net 60.

Businesses that offer discounts usually allow the customer to calculate the amount of the discount and subtract it from their payment. Modern credit software will often determine the discount for the customer and print it on the invoice. This translation from percentage to dollars makes a discount easier to understand and a bill easier to pay.

Savvy customers may try negotiating the discount by having it begin at the end of the month, not upon receipt of merchandise.

Key Terms:

- **C.I.A.**
  Cash in Advance

- **Net Wire Transfer**
  Good Funds Wire is
  Required

- **Net on Receipt of
  Invoice**
  Due Five Days After
  Invoice

- **Net xx Days**
  Due xx Days After
  Invoice

- **xx% 10 Days, Net 30**
  Discount Offered

- **Day After Delivery**
  Due Two Days After
  Invoice

- **Net 30 Days**
  Due 30 Days After
  Invoice

- **Net xx Prox**
  Due xx Day of Month
  Following

- **Net 10 Days (ACH)**
  ACH Net 10 Draft
  Terms

This maneuver gives a customer, on average, another 15 days to find the money to pay their bill with a discount. Like many of these issues, whether you agree to this term is a function of the overall relationship and value to your company.

A disturbing trend in the business world has customers taking a discount even when paying outside the discount period. With proper documentation, a business can legally collect these "unearned discounts." Whether or not you want to pursue unearned discounts depends on the customer's importance to your business and their relationship with you.

3. Late fees: Tacking on a fee to past due accounts is identified by a variety of names: *late payment charge, service charge, interest* or simply *late fee.* Our clients have recently noticed their own disturbing trend: larger companies are now stretching out payments far beyond the agreed terms and then ignoring late charges. Net 30 often becomes net 60—or longer. Remember that late fees are enforceable even when the customer pays the balance and, when large enough, may warrant collection and legal action.

Short of that, some companies respond to non-paid late fees by holding future orders, reducing the customer's credit limit, changing an open account to cash, or closing the account entirely.

For late fees to work they need company policies and culture that support consistent and fair enforcement. Policy should include when the fee starts, how much it is (a percentage or flat fee) and who can grant an exception and why. Late fees typically begin when an account is 30 days past due. Authority to hear—and possibly act on—requests for exceptions may be given to credit department managers or senior executives.

Common sense will probably tell you when a late charge should be waived. Examples where a waiver would make sense: if a very good customer is late by a few days or if a growing customer tells you in advance that a problem will cause a 10-day delay in payment and then pays within that period.

Discounts, late fees and credit limits are key components of an exclusive type of business relationship, the **open account**.

With an open account, approved customers order goods with or without a purchase order; no down payment is generally required. For discussion purposes, assume the purchase amounts to $1,000 and the terms are 2/10 net 30. Sellers then ship the product and bill the customer after the goods are shipped. Customers then pay either the full price less any discount in 10 days ($1,000 X .02 = $20; $1,000 - $20 = $980) or the full price ($1,000) in 30 days.

With an open account there are no fixed payments over months or years like a car loan. There is no large current balance that a debtor "pays down" in installments like a credit card. An open account is what Wimpy had with his hamburger supplier: his hamburger arrived today and he paid in full on Tuesday. Many of our nation's utilities follow this model. If you have a $50 water bill, you pay the $50 when the bill arrives. If you delay, there is a late fee. If you delay further, your water is turned off.

Open accounts and discounts are not without their own unique problems. One in particular—the start and end dates of the discount period—causes misunderstanding, hard feelings and conflict.

Credit agreements often specify that the discount period starts the day goods arrive at the customer's location. The seller's credit personnel assume the discount period begins the day they prepare the invoice. Customers have a third, fourth and sometimes a fifth date in mind: the date the invoice is received at the front desk, when it is logged in by accounts receivable or a negotiated date like the first of the month.

Which is correct? The short answer is whatever date the seller's policy specifies. The seller must have control over its own discounts and due dates, but the start and end dates have to be effectively and repeatedly communicated. Here are a few ways to accomplish that:

- Include the discount period and final due dates in a letter of confirmation.
- Print the words, "Please pay this invoice by (the 30th day)" on the invoice.
- Manually or electronically calculate the discount in dollars and add this statement to the invoice in bold large type: "To receive the 2 percent early-pay discount, pay $(selling price minus discount) by (date)."

- Make it easy for customers to pay in 10 days by sending invoices on the fifteenth of the month. It's often a good idea to ensure that their end of the month payment cycle and your discount period coincide.
- For negotiated start dates, make the negotiator responsible for getting that information to billing.

Because the date of delivery may be difficult to integrate into a billing system, we recommend starting everything with the date the invoice is prepared. It is an easily understood "seller controlled" date and one automatically included on all invoices. It is a better choice than any other option.

D. Invoicing Issues

Besides clarifying the discount start and end dates, there are a number of ways to improve billing. All have two interrelated goals: increasing customer understanding and improving customer relations.

We recommend:

1. Making it easy for a customer with only one document in front of them — your invoice — to contact someone who can help solve billing issues. To accomplish this, make sure the invoice includes your company's name, address, phone number and Web site as well as the name, phone number and e-mail address of a contact person. The more contact options, the better.

2. Including these vital statistics:

- Order date
- Product number and description
- Quantity ordered
- Delivery location
- Expected delivery date
- Purchase order number
- Name of the person who placed the order
- Date invoice prepared

3. Benefiting from the experience of nonprofit fundraisers. Make sure the customer knows who or what goes after "Pay to the order of . . ." on their check. Add this statement to the invoice along with a return envelope: "Make your check payable to . . . "

4. Including your late fee interest-charging policy. Use large bold type for the statement: "Interest at the rate of __ percent per year (__ percent per month) will accrue on all balances not paid within ___ days from the date of this invoice." Check applicable state law for maximum interest on late payments. Rates vary across the country from 5 percent to 18 percent, but also depend on whether the "borrower" is an individual or a corporation.

- When the bold print on an invoice confirms what's on a signed credit agreement, late fees are enforceable. If, on impulse, you approved a small order over the phone from a new customer who never signed an agreement and then months later asks forgiveness for paying late, your preferred late fee may be unenforceable. Technically, terms on an invoice (not seen prior to placing the order) may not be part of the

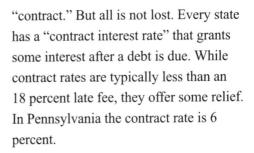

"contract." But all is not lost. Every state has a "contract interest rate" that grants some interest after a debt is due. While contract rates are typically less than an 18 percent late fee, they offer some relief. In Pennsylvania the contract rate is 6 percent.

- In general, it is a good idea to have *all* of your credit terms on the invoice. While they may not always be enforceable, they gently inform customers how you prefer doing business.

5. Listing all "No charge" items.

Customers enjoy knowing that there are some things in life that their vendors are doing *for* them (not *to* them). Keeping the freebies in front of them can take some of the sting out of writing the check.

6. Saying "Thank you." Waitresses,
waiters and local charities are repeatedly thanking people. We can learn from them. Saying "Thank you" is not painful and it's one of those small niceties that can make a huge difference.

7. Considering the benefits of the
Internet. Americans refer to the U.S. Postal
Service as "snail mail" for good reason.

Postal delays cut into a customer's discount period and increase frustration, conflict and the human and financial cost of resolving frustration and conflict. Web-based applications can speed and modernize billing and generally smooth your relationship with customers. For many companies, the Internet has become the preferred way of ordering goods, paying for them and capturing discounts.

- The field of business-to-business Electronic Invoice Presentment and Payment (EIPP) has grown significantly in the past few years. Some companies offer comprehensive software with tech support. Others are outsourcing entities.

- For more information, Google "EIPP" or visit the nonprofit National Automated Clearing House Association Web site, www.nacha.org.

While these invoice recommendations may appear to be common sense, some companies fail to implement them. We're not the first to observe that many collection problems can be traced to incomplete or inconsiderate invoices. Sellers who fix these problems improve their business relationships and their bottom line. Sometimes simple remedies can yield major benefits.

E. Reviewing Accounts

Every few years, my credit card company sends me a letter that does not ask for money. It says, in essence, they have reviewed my payment history and account activity and have raised my credit limit. I like receiving that letter. While I may never need the generous limits they allow, the letter tells me someone is looking at my account and, like my mother, keeping an eye on me.

Every year your company should review all of its credit accounts, not just the major ones or the marginal ones. It's surprising what changes can occur in 12 short months. As part of establishing a credit conscious culture, I recommend updating all of the review and investigation procedures we discussed in this chapter for all accounts. That includes checking the white and yellow pages of the telephone directory, calling bank, trade and competitor references, obtaining credit reports and checking with your professional colleagues.

Good idea, right? Of course it is. But you'd be surprised at how few companies take the time for any review. Yes, it takes some additional time and effort, but it can pay huge dividends in customer relations and collected sales.

Decide to be an exceptional enterprise and begin now to sow the seeds of change.

Here are a few ways to begin the process:

- Review accounts in the month of their anniversary date. With luck, that will distribute accounts somewhat evenly throughout the year.
- Ask sales and credit personnel for their input on the accounts to be reviewed each month.
- Check on each customer's payment history, average number of days late and the age of their account.
- Include the controller in the review. Supply her with current financial statements for all accounts to be reviewed.
- Provide reviewers with benchmark data. One of the most common is Days Sales Outstanding (DSO), a statistic usually calculated quarterly. A low DSO means the company is quickly collecting its receivables. A high DSO indicates credit sales have increased and it's taking longer to collect the company's money. Like miles per hour, DSO is a measure of speed, not quality or effectiveness.

DSO = Current end-of-month accounts
receivable X 90
Total sales for the past three months

For example, if at the end of June receivables were $20,000 and total sales for April, May and June were $30,000, the ratio would be:

$$DSO = \frac{\$20{,}000 \times 90}{\$30{,}000} = 60 \text{ days}$$

If policy allows for a 30-day term, a DSO of 60 means it's taking the company twice that time to collect on its debts. Ideal DSO should run no more than 10 to 15 days over the terms of sale.

If at the end of September receivables were $10,000 on July-September sales of $25,000, DSO would be lower than the previous quarter and just six days over the terms of sale.

$$DSO = \frac{\$10{,}000 \times 90}{\$25{,}000} = 36 \text{ days}$$

One of the claims of the EIPP industry is that by harnessing the lightning-fast Internet, a company would experience a reduction in its DSO. They are right—in general. Any method that makes it easier for customers to pay should reduce DSO.

Another useful measure is "average days delinquent," which shows delinquent accounts receivable, taking into account varying credit terms.

In science, law and credit, the old adage applies: Data wins. Updated financials, current payment history and revised bank and trade references are the credit manager's best data. Winning comes from effectively combining the numbers and deciding to increase or decrease a customer's credit limit.

Saying "thanks" to customers who pay on time may also encourage that behavior. Systems can automatically generate an email or letter when a customer payment comes in on time. We feel good when we get thanked or congratulated. It makes us want to repeat the behavior.

F. Anticipating Red Zone Problems

As part of the assessment, there may be indicators that a potential customer might be a "Red Zone" risk. Here are a few indicators that might signal the need for a credit limit reduction:

- A change in a customer's good standing at their bank.
- An increase in the number of bank loans and failure to pay as agreed.
- Business references report an increase in average days late or the age of the customer's account.
- Small claims judgments on the updated credit reports.
- Management changes. This comes back to the "character" issue. Changes in the respect bankers, industry leaders and analysts have for the current leadership. This sort of information comes from knowing your customer and the industry. It can also be gleaned from business publications and from periodic reference checks.
- Changes in current bank balances or the number and types of bank accounts.

- Troubling changes in the customer's current financial statements. For example, reduction in net worth, operational losses and increases in short-term debt.

Credit managers who decide to decrease a customer's credit limit might want to go the extra mile when breaking the bad news. Face-to-face discussions may be difficult, but there is much to be learned—and salvaged—from life's awkward moments. Here are the steps we recommend, along with some of the advantages of an in-office "bad news" conversation:

- **Don't delay.** The sooner you inform the client of a problem, the sooner he can get to work fixing it. Let him know before he places an order that it will be rejected. Schedule these conversations early in the day. Like ripping off a band-aid, it's best to get unpleasant tasks over with fast.

- **Tell the truth.** Explain what went into the decision and what the decision is. Emphasize the objectivity of the decision. Avoid injecting personal sentiment such as, "I'm sorry."

- **Wait for a response.** How the customer responds says a lot about her or his character. Some deny the problem and make light of it. Others shift the blame to others or to your firm. Still others get emotional. A few accept the news and express regret. Whatever the reaction, it usually validates your decision to decrease the limits.

- **Offer solutions.** Come to the conversation equipped with ideas for getting the business relationship back on track. Offer a life preserver, not false, unrealistic hope in a dreamy future where everything has magically changed. Look at possible credit enhancements such as a personal guarantee, a lien against merchandise or a letter of credit. These standard business tools might turn the conversation from bad news to a win-win outcome.

- **Wait and see.** Offer assurances that the account will be reviewed again in a year—or possibly sooner. If there are improvements in the customer's business and payment habits, you'll take them into account at the next review.

It's a good idea to memorialize the conversation and any agreements in a letter or email after the discussion. Breaking good news such as announcing an increase in the customer's credit limit is easier and simpler: send a letter.

Does all this sound like a lot of work up front? Frankly, it is. But it's time well spent. If you're ever tempted to skip the "A" step in the GET P.A.I.D. System, just remember the grandmotherly proverb "A stitch in time saves nine." (Those grandmothers were a pretty wise bunch!)

Thoroughly investigating credit applicants is the "stitch" that can prevent a lot of costly unraveling of customer relationships down the road. Do it now and you'll be glad later.

Implementation
Collections Strategy and Procedures

chapter 4

There is a lot of good news and some bad news in this chapter. The good news is that about 95% of commercial customers pay their bills when they are due. That figure has dropped from the late 1990s when it was close to 98%, but it is still high enough to qualify as good news. When a company bills, most customers pay. However, the longer a company waits to collect payment from that troublesome 5%, the less likely they are to collect.

The bad news is that collecting from the other 5% takes effort and a company is going to pay for it in staff time and frustration. We'll spend a lot of time in this book on that 5% and so will most companies.

Why so much attention to 5%? Because it could include some of a firm's largest accounts and the difference between business success and failure. That raises the ante on collecting.

A. Persistence Pays

A man walks into his doctor's office to get a report on his recent tests. The doctor says, "I have some good news and bad news for you, Bill." "Give me the good news first," says Bill nervously. The doctor smiles and says, "My daughter's just been accepted at Harvard Law." "That's great. What's the bad news," asks Bill. Still smiling, the doctor says, "You're going to pay her tuition."

We'll also spend time in this chapter on ways to make collections easier, more efficient and less like paying tuition at Harvard Law.

Collecting is not the same as billing. Billing is paperwork mixed with inducements for paying on time. Consider the Three P's of Collecting. It's part *Policy*, part *Psychology* and part *Persistence*. Collecting is more art than science but can be as delicate as brain surgery.

Re-examine Chart 1.1 and 1.2 in Chapter 1 to appreciate the first rule of collecting: **Act quickly**. The longer a company waits to contact its late paying customers, the worse the situation gets.

How quickly should a company act on collections? During the first 90 days after the due date. It is a company's window of greatest opportunity. Add that to the typical 30-day grace period and the window is a mere 120 days – four short months from invoice. That is all the time a successful collection program should run. After that, we recommend placing delinquent accounts with a collection professional.

If that timetable seems too fast and unusually cruel, consider some of the costs involved.

Late payments ripple through the organization, delaying a company's ability to pay its business loans or meet its own obligations such as operating expenses or distributions to owners. Besides its effect on the bottom line, late payments have associated emotional costs. Employees worry about whether the company will ever get paid. Worry develops into fear that delinquencies will trickle down and jeopardize jobs and livelihood. And when they have to constantly remind slow payers to meet their obligations, employees feel like parents nagging unruly teenagers. That breeds resentment, a cost that changes employees' tone of voice, poisons their attitude and eventually reduces good customer service.

Rarely discussed are the costs of late payments on debtors. Owing money is stressful; it's like a death in the family – it happens to everyone, but we still have a hard time acknowledging it. Debt can reduce or stop business and social contacts, ruin a customer's credit rating and place future sales to that client in jeopardy. It makes late payers feel like credit criminals which they are not.

Robert's Rules of Credit

*All things considered, creditors have an obligation to turn "slow and late payers" into "as agreed payers." It is good for the company **and** good for customers*

Also factor in human nature. The longer someone owes you money, the more difficult it is for them to part with it. If you ever owed parents or relatives money, you realize how easy it is to put them at the bottom of your payment priority list. You don't want customers to do that to you.

B. Avoiding The Red Zone: 10 Steps To Progressive Collection

Collection is a process, not an event. It progresses from a reminder to initiation of legal remedy. Here is a suggested timetable for acting quickly on late payments. It's based on our firm's experience with our clients.

1. Customer Service call

Call the customer within a week after delivery, but before payment is due. Separate and apart from the goodwill it engenders, this call has several important purposes: It

• Opens a discussion about whether the product conforms to the customer's order, and hopefully can avoid a later claim by the customer that they did not get what they ordered.

• Allows the customer to air any problems with the shipment or product and the company to correct the problem. This can help prevent the later use of a claim of a defective product as an attempt to justify non-payment.

• Reminds the customer of the date when payment in full is expected and that you are closely following the transaction and will be expecting timely payment.

Be sure to document the contact, as well as the customer's comments, in the customer's file or in the comment section of your billing software. Include the date and time of the call, who initiated the call, who participated and what was said. Ideally, the contact should be from the salesperson who made the sale. Second best would be a "Quality Control" person.

With new or large accounts, a customer visit might take the place of a courtesy call. Corporate cultures that strongly support credit and collections also see the value of meeting customers face to face. Visits or calls may be scheduled early in the relationship or later. If later, be sure to come prepared with more than a firm handshake and a smile. Know the details of the customer's account such as when payments were due and missed and the content of previous conversations between the customer and credit personnel. While there, take a good look around to notice things that might add to any review or assessment of the credit. Visits are expensive, but always worth it.

The letter of confirmation, a credit enhancement discussed in Chapter 2, may take the place of a sales follow-up call or visit.

2. Payment reminder
(Invoice due date + 10 days)

Ten days after the invoice due date, call, fax or send an e-mail, to remind the customer that payment is due. The objective is straight forward: Remind the customer that the money is due using the most direct, effective and polite means possible.

Surprisingly, a reminder may be all that is needed. "A word to the wise is sufficient," applies to some late paying customers. Ask them if the product met their needs and was delivered on time. Then remind them that the bill is due and that you expect payment in full. Many pay after this simple reminder. Sometimes, invoices really do get lost in the paperwork.

This first contact may be the single most important communication you will have with a late payer. Keep it friendly, but businesslike; firm, but concerned about the customer's satisfaction with the product and the company. Entrust only those employees who are skilled in customer relations with this first, critical contact, rather than a "take no prisoners" collector. Their role comes later.

Every civic club I ever joined reminded me that the only way to get a new member was to ask someone. Few deliberately join Rotary or Kiwanis. The same simple rule applies to late payers.

3. Request for payment
(Invoice due date + 20 days)

Wait 10 days. If payment has not arrived, write and then call the customer. Enclose another copy of the invoice, but stamp it "past due." When you call, keep the tone friendly and non-threatening, but business-like. "Did you receive the duplicate invoice? Was it overlooked? When can I expect payment? Can you send it today?" This time, specifically ask for the money. You have already sent them the reminder. At this point, it's not a question of forgetting or losing the invoice.

4. First demand letter and call
(Invoice due date + 30 days)

Wait 10 more days. If no payment is received, send a demand letter to the debtor. Now the customer has become a debtor. Send the demand letter by certified mail, demonstrating to the debtor that you are establishing a "paper trail" for your communications. The purpose now changes from friendly to firm.

Within a week after you send the demand letter, place your first "demand call." As you prepare for this call, remember that there are compelling reasons for a delayed payment. They range from the personal – sickness, accident, death, divorce, bankruptcy – to the professional – natural disaster, theft, business downturns, loss of a major client, law suits. Be prepared for reasons, excuses and hard luck stories. Also be prepared to be hardnosed about payment. Choose your words, tone of voice and volume carefully.

Here are a few specific actions you can take as a matter of course in your business while the debtor is still a customer. Laying the groundwork can help make this critical conversation work:

- **Develop a personal relationship** between the accounts payable manager of your largest customer and your accounts receivable manager. A friendly relationship that includes lunch and sharing information about family and hobbies makes every interaction easier. The voice on the other end of the phone is now an acquaintance, possibly a friend.

- **Review past communications.** Check the comments section of billing software, review the debtor's file and refresh your understanding of the credit agreement and company policy. Familiarize yourself with what happened in prior contacts with the debtor.

- **Resolve to maintain your composure.** Counselors who are about to undergo difficult conversations often stop, put their hand over their heart and take a deep breath. Some say a prayer. Then they open the counseling room door and benefit from their routine. Here is a suggested statement you can say aloud before a collection call:

"I am not going to take this conversation personally or feel sorry for the debtor. I am not going to argue, interrupt, evaluate or lose my temper. This debtor owes us money, and they will pay us. I am in control of myself and this situation. My goal is to find a solution the debtor can live with, not impose a solution."

- **Ask to speak to the owner**, chief financial officer or someone having decision making authority. Don't waste time and effort with low level accounts payable clerks. They simply print out the checks once payment decisions are made. They only do what the boss tells them and that rarely includes authorizing payment.

- **Identify yourself and your company.** Then state the purpose of your call ("The XYZ account with ABC Company is delinquent and must be paid now").

- **State the amount of the debt and then provide some choices**, not ultimatums. The debt can be paid now or tomorrow, by check or credit card. "Payment can be delivered here today by courier or someone from this office can come over before the close of business to pick up a check."

- **Wait and listen.** Now it's the debtor's turn. Be silent. As the debtor responds, keep the conversation going with "Um hmmm," "I see," or "I understand." Rarely in life are we ever genuinely understood. If this step is done authentically by someone who feels confident in the role of bill collector, the next steps flow naturally.

- **What's the problem?** Did you learn what is holding up payment? There may not be a hold up - the debtor may accept payment responsibility and send a check today by courier. Or there may be a big problem – the debtor refuses to pay. In between "Yes" and "No" are objections or a dispute over the product or terms.

- **Work toward a solution**. See yourself on the debtor's side. The two of you are trying to find a way to get this bill paid.

If the problem has to do with a dispute over merchandise, service, price or delivery, work especially hard to resolve it quickly. By raising a dispute, credit criminals lob the ball into your court and hope it stays there. If your best efforts to resolve a dispute fail, this may be an account for a collection agency or attorney.

If there is an objection to payment such as "I don't have the money," remember that an objection is the *customer's* reason for not buying or in this case, not paying. That reason can be changed by acknowledging the objection, restating it in your own words, answering it and selling the debtor on a way to overcome it. If the debtor hangs on to the objection, try a little sympathy. Get on the customer's side and try again to find a way out. Remember your telephone mantra: "I am not going to argue, interrupt, evaluate or lose my temper."

Keep the focus on payment alternatives. There are a number of tools available to the debtor that might work: cash advance on a personal credit card, selling or bartering assets, borrowing from a bank, postdating a check, returning the merchandise. There are also tools provided by credit enhancements such as personal guarantee, lien against merchandise and letter of credit that were discussed in Chapter 2.

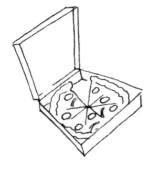

There are also tools that are based on time such as extended payments or partial payments. In general, discourage extended payments. Most of the nation's largest retailers have eliminated "layaway." You should too. Furthermore, outside of normal credit terms, you don't want to be a long-term lender. You are not in the business of servicing debt. Any allowance for partial payments should be coupled with a specific promise of final payment. The two go together like pepperoni pizza and calories – you can't have the first one without the second.

If the customer refuses to pay, indicates that he or she does not abide by your terms of sale or steadfastly resists finding a solution, it may be best to move the process along faster. The follow-up letter discussed in Step 5 may need to contain a summary of your conversation *and* an early referral to a collection professional.

- **Don't overlook the calming effect of humor.** Jokes, offhand comments or humorous comparisons help relax people. When we laugh, we escape from or minimize life's problems.

- **Solidify the solution:** How, when and where need to be determined. Exact times, dates and amounts are the rule.

- **Paperwork:** Update the file or comments section in your billing software with promised dates and amounts and who participated in the solution discussion.

5. Confirming letter
(Invoice due date + 45 days)

This letter is part of the paperwork that confirms the discussions with the debtor and hopefully the solutions you negotiated and agreed upon. Outline the solution, promises, dates, times and amounts. Send it to the debtor the next day. Better yet, put a space at the bottom of the letter for the debtor to sign to confirm his agreement with the solutions you reached, and include a self-addressed stamped envelope for him to return the counter-signed letter to you. Another option to consider is e-mail, which allows the debtor to do an easy response, thereby confirming receipt.

6. Escalated efforts
(Invoice due date + 60 days)

If after waiting 10 days there is still no payment or the counter-signed letter is not received, then have a trained, in-house collector make a second collection call.

Follow the routine outlined in Step 4. The collector should be firm, but not rude, and should specifically ask for the money. The collector should maintain regular contact with the debtor, and should be persistent with regular calls, and probably visits, but should not let this phase of the collection process go beyond 30 days.

7. Upper management involvement and self-help (Invoice due date + 90 days)

So the collector has been making efforts to collect for 30 days. No payment? It's time for stronger action, demonstrating your assertiveness and emphasizing the urgency of the situation. Everything at this step is meant to increase pressure on the debtor. At this point, upper management should get involved in the process. A senior member of your company should call, or better yet, arrange a visit with the debtor's upper management to stress the seriousness of the situation. Also, the debtor should be reminded about the effect this delinquency will have on his credit rating and about the possibility of legal action. If your transaction with the debtor provided for some self-help remedies, for example, re-possession, and if you retained a security interest in the products you sold on credit, you should seriously consider pursuing such remedies and so inform the debtor.

Immediately after upper management's phone call and/or visit with the debtor's upper management, a final demand letter should be sent, under the signature of your chief executive officer, chief financial officer or credit manager. Demand payment within 10 days or the account will be reviewed for placement with a collection firm.

Books have been written on the fine points of collection letters. Save time by checking with the collection professional you've retained. They may have a letter writing service or be able to help with suggestions.

For other third-party collection letter forms, refer to our resource guides on getpaidsystem.com

8. Final collection call (Invoice due date + 100 days)

Wait 10 days. Review Step 4 and demand the money one more time.

9. Final Warning

Fax, e-mail or call to alert the debtor that
you are packaging the account for placement
unless payment is received within the next
24 hours.

10. Collection agent referral
(Invoice due date + 114 days)

Do what you said you would do. For many
late payers, a demand letter or phone call from
an outside collector takes the debtor to a new
"threshold of pain" that has greater effect than
your phone calls and letters. Referral to an
outside agent is not "a last resort." It is instead
a carefully determined intention established
in company policy. There will be more on
collection agencies and collection law firms in
Chapter 6.

After reviewing the 10-step schedule,
company leaders usually have one of two
reactions: "Sounds OK to me," or "I don't
have the staff to effectively operate such a
system. What are the alternatives?"

For those that find the 10 steps OK, we need
to add a few caveats. Businesses that sell
products to consumers for personal, family

Get P.A.I.D.

A Guide to Getting Paid Faster (and What To Do If You Don't!)

or household use need to be aware of the Fair Debt Collection Practices Act (FDCPA), as well as the debtor's state's consumer protection statutes and regulations. The FDCPA and most state consumer protection statutes and regulations cover agencies collecting consumer debt, not businesses working to collect their own debts. Some state consumer protection statutes and regulations do cover businesses collecting their own debts. Such statutes and regulations do not apply to collection of commercial debts. Nevertheless, credit criminals will accuse *any* bill collector of harassment, unfair practices or making false statements, activities made illegal by FDCPA. Under the right circumstances (such as a sole proprietor debtor or a personal guarantor of a corporate debt) credit criminals will even try to "spin" the situation and invoke the protections of the FDCPA and other consumer protection statutes and regulations, in the collection of a commercial debt. It is wise to follow the act's intent and spirit when collecting either commercial or consumer debts while understanding that most harassment law suits are the hot air of school yard bullies who have aged a few years. Plaintiffs have to prove damages in court and establish that the purpose of the underlying debt was goods or services primarily for

personal family or household use. Most who claim harassment are people who are not adept at follow-through. They don't pay their bills or hire an attorney. Bottom line: don't abuse debtors, but don't be afraid of their threats of law suits either.

Staffing a company-managed collection department means hiring, training and supervising some highly talented individuals. Credit/collections specialists are skilled professionals. They know how to communicate, negotiate, mediate and organize their work. Some employers set the entry level for this key position at the bachelor's level with majors in business, accounting or finance. Even with academic preparation, many employers send their collection staff to the local community college for a course specifically designed for credit and collections specialists. Others train their own.

Even a company with an aggressive in-house collections department usually includes a "failure cushion" or bad debt reserve in its annual budget. If the reserve is estimated accurately, net income is not reduced when debts are written off as uncollectible. Although businesses are usually guided by past performance in estimating the reserve, economic conditions need to be factored into the equation. Bad debts are inversely related to the economy. When times are good, bad debt decreases. When the economy falters, bad debt increases.

For businesses that find a 10-step collections schedule beyond the capability of their staff, there is a relatively new service that eases the burden. Outsourcing takes a non-core business function, like customer service or collections, and places it with a group of specialists.

My friend Dave owns one of a number of companies that specialize in credit and collection outsourcing. He finds American businesses increasingly receptive to outsourcing. "Companies are involved in a shift to a new economy - a new age - a new way and approach to doing business. Things are shifting more and more to services and expert knowledge work," said Dave. "Before long, top management absolutely won't be able to run things the old way, even if they wanted to. There is no one to blame for this. But, we jeopardize our future if we cling to old assumptions and expectations." He added, "In five to 10 years I expect we'll see two-thirds of the white-collar labor force self-employed through outsourcing companies."

For those familiar with a much older form of accounts receivable management, he said, "Outsourcing has nothing to do with factoring." In factoring, a company sells its accounts receivable at a discount in order to raise funds. The sold accounts are transferred to the factoring organization, which collects in the name of the original business or under its own name. Nothing is sold in outsourcing. The collections function is merely handed off to specialists for a fee.

"It is cheaper for companies to buy the expertise than build it themselves," said Dave. That's an advantage that appeals to companies too small to afford their own credit and collections specialists. He listed some of the other outsourcing advantages: reduced DSO, improved cash flow, earlier handling of customer accounts, improved communication and lower hiring, training and benefit costs.

Visit www.bernsteinlaw.com to find additional firms that specialize in collections outsourcing.

In summary, delinquent accounts receivable are not like fine wine. They do not improve with age. The longer you take to act on collecting your delinquent accounts receivable, the less likely you are to collect them in full. Look at Chart 1.1 in Chapter 1 again. The figures don't lie.

Defense
Defending Your Policy

Clear, reasonable policies "on the books" and "in the minds" of collections personnel beat no policies or policies that are weak or ignored. Weak or absent credit policies are key ingredients in a recipe for trouble.

We have just finished reviewing our preferred method for handling collections - a 10-point plan that escalates from friendly to firm. We believe in the plan. It allows for both gentle nudges and firm shoves. Reasonable slow payers get the message, and we recommend the plan as a guide for a company's collection policy. But we must caution against slavishly relying on its 10 points. There are circumstances when the plan needs to be massaged and collector is allowed to embark on an alternative plan. Persistence pays, but sometimes so does flexibility.

A. Act Decisively

Mark Twain may have been on to something when he advised: "If at first you don't succeed, try, try again. Then give up. There's no sense being a damn fool about it."

We recommend following Twain's advice. Give the 10-step plan a good try. Go as far as Step 8 – the invoice date plus 100 days and then check the list of danger signs below.

With that information under your belt, you may want to reconsider taking Step 9. Also take a good hard look at what's learned at Step 7. That may also be a good "give up" point. After upper management has become involved and gathered its own information, a mid-plan collection correction may be in order.

When slow pays turn into no pays, there are usually warning signs. Here are the most common signs we advise our clients to heed. If three or more of these questions are answered "Yes," regroup and try a new strategy:

- Is the owner or responsible party never able to come to the phone?
- Are telephone messages not returned?
- Are telephone messages returned promptly, but without a payment commitment or new information?
- Have new orders ceased or slowed to a trickle?
- Does the customer harass your staff with unfounded complaints and arguments?
- Do annual credit reports show evidence of legal suits or judgments?
- Has the telephone been disconnected?
- Is mail being returned?

- Is certified mail unclaimed?
- Has the debtor moved?
- Have you received a bankruptcy notice?

The first six danger signs hold out hope that the debtor is still in business, but avoiding his or her creditors. The second five are more serious and require more drastic steps. Some steps are addressed here while others are covered later in Chapters 6 and 7.

So, what new strategies are available in the face of danger? A creditor can:

- Redouble in-house collection efforts.
- Move up the timetable for referral to a collection professional.
- Call for legal help.

**Robert's
Rules of Credit**

*Strategies
For Ratcheting Up
The Pressure*

1. *Insider Reports*

2. *Credit Enhancements*

3. *A Lien Against
Merchandise*

4. *Letters of Credit*

5. *Collection Agency
or Attorney*

6. *Collection Agencies*

7. *Calling For
Legal Help*

8. *Purchase Money
Security Interest*

B. The Red Zone: 10 Strategies for Ratcheting Up The Pressure

With the company now in real danger of not collecting on its debt, the collection staff must increase debtor pressure and accelerate the transition from friendly to firm. "Firm" means stopping deliveries, placing a hold on all credit, adding the penalty interest rate to overdue accounts, sending the sales representative to make a visit and enforcing any credit enhancements.

Stopping deliveries and placing a hold on all future credit are clear messages, but they must be loud, too. Make sure the customer's owner, chief financial officer or anyone else in authority is copied with the letter or e-mail announcing the change from business-as-usual. Cite the warning signs you observed, express your concern and ask for full payment immediately.

Before increasing interest on an overdue account, creditors need to make sure that the tactic is covered in the late fee section of their credit agreement. Hardened No Pays will ignore the higher rate, but having the new percentage on the record provides some leverage later for collection professionals and creditors' rights attorneys.

To a delinquent debtor, a visit from a creditor's sales rep is part business, part personal. For the creditor, the visit is all business. But remind the sales rep to maintain composure. Review our discussion of finding a solution the debtor can live with in Chapter 4. A sales representative needs to bring three simple, direct, anger-free messages to the debtor: "There are serious business consequences to a credit hold and delivery stoppage. Even a small bad debt can damage your credit rating for years to come. You will incur a substantial financial burden if this goes to court."

It is a good idea to prepare the sales rep with as much information as possible before the visit. A review of the debtor's credit report, payment record and collection department's efforts in following the collection plan are good for starters. In recent years, many collection departments have also armed anyone visiting a delinquent account with the debtor's CEO's personal cell phone number. Few interventions are as surprising as hearing from a creditor on a private, personal telephone line.

1. Insider Reports

Until 2006, cell phone numbers and calling records were available from a number of companies as part of what were known as insider reports or national profiles. These documents were filled with personal data obtained from multiple sources. A CEO's Social Security number – possibly available from your credit agreement - was all that was needed to begin the process of compiling his or her insider report. In early 2006, the Missouri attorney general cracked down on insider report companies operating in his state. He charged them with violating state privacy laws and prevented them from selling the cell phone records of Missouri citizens.

Hearings on the federal level soon followed. Legislators linked the selling of private cell phone records with identity theft, a hot button issue at all levels of the American electorate. Since police and private investigators must subpoena cell phone records, making them available to creditors for $150 raised a number of concerns. Given the federal government's history of shielding debtors from harassment, national legislation protecting cell phone records is not unexpected.

2. Questionable Collection Tactics

Despite its bad reputation some people think tough treatment of credit criminals is one of the most effective means of getting paid. Punishing debtors by repeatedly disrupting their business, damaging their equipment or photographing them in contrived, embarrassing situations are dirty tricks that some think get results. Although you should know how hardcore collectors work, our law firm does not recommend any of these practices.

Those who are good at dirty tricks take great pains to stay anonymous. They use surrogates to deliver messages, distribute false discount coupons, hide a dead animal in a show room, disconnect critical electrical plugs, fill locks with superglue, spill soft drinks on computers and collect payments. Their workers come cheap: $50 to a homeless person buys a lot of disruption. Collectors who specialize in dirty tricks might work for 50% of outstanding debts in the $2,000 to $15,000 range. Their work is never personal. This is a low-key, no evidence, non-emotional business. If you saw the *Godfather* movies, you understand the mindset. Hardcore collectors have reacted to Congress making harassment illegal by becoming extra cautious and creative. The law has not put them out of business.

3. Pretexting

Those who compiled insider reports used different tactics. They posed as cell phone customers requesting their own record. When their impersonation raises a red flag, they simply redial and ask the next operator for the same information. Eventually, they obtain what they were looking for. This is an example of pretexting, a practice the Federal Trade Commission defines as obtaining personal information under false pretenses. Pretexting is illegal under the Gramm-Leach-Bliley Act. You cannot use false, fictitious or fraudulent statements or documents to obtain customer information from a financial institution or from that institution's customers. It is also against the law to use forged, counterfeit, lost or stolen documents to obtain information. And it is illegal to recruit another person to get the information with false, fraudulent or stolen statements or documents.

4. Credit Enhancements

Credit enhancements are added protections, often written into your credit agreement (see Chapter 2). They provide legal access to the debtor's capital and financial infrastructure in case of default. With danger signs looming, this may be the time to take them out of the gun case. Included in this arsenal are a personal guarantee (or guaranty), a lien against property, letters of credit and a purchase money security interest. We also recommended a letter of confirmation, an enhancement that is sent to debtors shortly after goods are ordered. Confirmation letters becomes extremely useful if the case is litigated.

Enforcing credit enhancements requires, at various times, the help of the debtor's banker, your banker, your attorney and the state's secretary of state.

Most personal guaranty documents, like the one in your credit agreement, waive a debtor's right to be notified before a creditor takes legal action. Generally, these documents are enforced when a creditor makes a formal demand for payment from the guarantor (customer, now debtor). If not satisfied by the deadline, the creditor usually seeks legal relief.

5. A Lien against Merchandise

A security interest is a lien against personal property. For businesses, that generally means equipment, accounts receivable or inventory. It's relatively easy to initiate a security interest. Check with your attorney for the proper language and make it part of a standard credit agreement. Even though it's on paper, don't let your guard down. Enforcing a security agreement requires an understanding of the fine points of credit and commercial law.

Creditors with a security interest in merchandise they sold to a customer need to check on whether a bank or other lender has a prior interest in the customer's *entire* inventory. A prior interest means that the bank, not the creditor, has priority if the customer goes bankrupt.

There is a way around this problem if creditors do some work in advance of delivery. Without that additional work, as soon as the new merchandise is delivered, the security interest of the bank, where, for example, the customer went for a capital improvement loan, includes (or attaches to) the new delivery.

Here's what to do. If you give notice to the bank that you intend to ship to the customer and that you intend to take a purchase money security interest or PMSI on that delivery (more about PMSI in a few pages), your lien becomes the senior lien on that portion of the customer's inventory.

But this protection has another catch. It assumes that creditors know of the bank's prior lien. Even with a search of all security interest filings with the state's secretary of state, creditors might miss something. A true story will help illustrate. A lawn tractor dealer pledged its entire inventory to a bank as collateral for a loan. The bank filed all the proper forms with the secretary of state using the dealer's physical address. A supplier (appropriately) searched for any prior liens, but it used the dealer's mailing address, a post office box. When the supplier found no outstanding liens for that address, he sold the dealer $400,000 in inventory. The dealer never paid its bills and went bankrupt; the bank claimed the entire inventory and the supplier lost its $400,000.

6. Letters of Credit

There are a number of different types of letters of credit. They all involve the creditor's bank and your new best friend, the debtor's banker. The most common is the standby letter, a document issued by a bank on behalf of its customer. It provides assurances of the customer's ability to perform under the terms of a contract with you, the beneficiary. The customer and beneficiary do not expect that the letter of credit will ever be enforced. It is a credit safeguard. If the debtor defaults, a standby letter of credit obligates the debtor's bank to pay the beneficiary or the beneficiary's bank.

Sounds like easy street? Don't be fooled. Letters of credit may be required by your credit agreement, but it's your customer who requests the document from his or her bank. Make sure the terms of the Letter of Credit meet your approval. What steps do you have to take to get paid? Make sure they are what you expect. Typically when creditors receive the letter, they treat it like an insurance policy and simply file it. Avoid that misstep and internally circulate the letter among your business associates. Ask them to check the letter's expiration date. Is it realistic? Check for discrepancies such as missing documents that are listed in the letter, differences between the invoice amount and draft amount and inaccurate description of goods. Wise creditors accept a standby letter of credit that is irrevocable, dated, numbered, signed, written on the issuing bank's stationery and enforceable simply with copies of unpaid invoices.

7. Collection Agency or Attorney?

After the collections staff has ignited a fire under no-pay debtors, there may be no need for the second and third new strategy. But if issues remain unresolved, creditors are faced with a choice: "Should I turn next to a collection agency or creditors' rights attorney?"

The roles of the collection agency and creditors' rights attorney are discussed in detail in our next chapter. Our focus here is on deciding which to call for an early, danger-sign-related referral.

8. Collection Agencies

Like all businesses, collection agencies prefer long-term clients. And creditors faced with multiple delinquencies are prime client material. There are advantages in accepting multiple problem debtors from a single client. If a collection agency offers a "no collection, no cost" contingency arrangement, they increase their chances of success with more debtors. Their motto: "The more debtors from one client, the better."

For the creditor, on-going placements with an agency are also a good deal. Agencies may lower their fees for on-going clients, report on collection activities in bulk and develop a more collaborative relationship with the creditor. That relationship might not only increase collections, but may also give creditors new insight into any vexing credit administration problems they face. They may learn something from the pros. An agency's willingness to take on clients with multiple debtors is a clear advantage over a general practice attorney where one client with one large troublesome debtor is ideal.

Collection agencies can also have an advantage over the client's local lawyer when debtors are widely scattered across the country. Some agencies either have branches in major American cities or cooperative relationships with out-of-state members of various trade associations. They may be better equipped to deal with a diverse and far flung debtor pool than are general practice attorneys. Attorneys are often most efficient when debtors reside in the jurisdictions where they practice.

There are other advantages related to a collection agency's wide reach. An agency may combine your delinquent account in Cincinnati and discover that some of their other clients have trouble with the same account. That information may help change a fragmented, hit or miss collection into a coordinated attack.

Collection agencies are also like the man who sells pretzels on the street corner. Since pretzels are his specialty and sole means of support, he develops repeat business by being better than the competition and by adding extra services, condiments and varieties. Most general law practice offices cannot match the level of concentrated collection efforts offered by collection agencies. Collections are their specialty.

If a collection agency's dogged determination fails, if the debtor continues to avoid payment, and if no progress is made, the advantage shifts to the legal profession. That shift can be easily expedited; many collection agencies work closely with and refer clients to a creditors' rights attorney. When that time comes, you can also request a specific attorney.

9. Calling for legal help

An attorney is not always the second professional that creditors turn to when danger signs appear. When there are people who need to be sued and security interests involved, an attorney can be the better first choice.

Who needs to be sued? Generally, there are two debtor personalities that qualify. Those who enjoy delaying payment until creditors bring out the big guns – their attorney – and those who enjoy making it expensive for creditors to collect. The most egregious debtors are those that do both. Delaying suit just increases the time – and money – it will take to get paid.

We also recommend seeing an attorney first for creditors who have a lien that needs to be enforced. The security interest has become increasingly popular as protection in the last few years.

The downside for creditors is that there are hidden complexities to security interests. Is the debtor a corporation or a limited liability corporation? That and dozens of other issues need to be taken into account. There are also legal documents that have to be filed, deadlines met and documents renewed. In other words, without legal help it's easy to miss the details of a security interest either when they are initiated or later if they have to be enforced.

10. Purchase Money Security Interest

An important type of lien for creditors is the purchase money security interest or PMSI. Here is how it works. A new customer wants to buy a substantial amount of merchandise on credit. The seller is hesitant, but offers the buyer a choice: a small line of credit without a security interest or a higher line with a security interest. With more credit, the buyer is able to take possession of more merchandise. That makes the buyer – and the sales rep – happy and the arrangement is often accepted.

A PMSI is essentially a formal and complex lien against what the seller sells. By making the assets secure, a PMSI encourages the

seller to take a risk with a new, untested customer. Like any chattel paper, a PMSI can then be taken to the bank and financed to raise funds for the seller's business operations.

With the precautions we discussed earlier, a PMSI can give a creditor priority to reclaim its inventory in case of bankruptcy, but be careful. If the PMSI is broadened to include other assets in which the debtor has rights, not just merchandise purchased from the creditor, it may lose its special character. A security interest is not limited to the state where it was initiated and can reach across state lines and attach to merchandise or other collateral. It is a document that leaves nothing to chance. A PMSI security interest defines default, outlines creditor remedies and specifies costs that the debtor incurs if default occurs. It is such an important contract that it must be filed with the secretary of state where the debtor company has its principal office.

If you have a security interest or bond rights (also called a mechanic's lien) with a delinquent debtor and are not fluent in legalese, check with an attorney first.

C. Case Studies

Here are some examples of how clients got paid by acting decisively.

1. Collecting After Bankruptcy

A client of ours was an unsecured creditor owed $300,000 by a customer with about $500,000 in assets. Unless it found some cash, the customer was going to go out of business. Although no institution would lend to the customer under those circumstances, the customer was willing to give our client a security interest for the $300,000. There was a risk: if the customer failed and went into bankruptcy, the bankruptcy trustee could undo (avoid) our security interest. We learned that it would take $100,000 for the customer to remain viable for the next several months. We negotiated a security interest for the $100,000 and a separate, junior security interest for the $300,000 plus interest and attorney's fees. When the customer filed for bankruptcy, the trustee ruled that our client's security interests were not preferential transfers and allowed them to stand.

As a result, our client was able to get paid in full on both loans from the inventory and other assets.

2. Documentation Pays

Another client sold to a steel company customer "on consignment" — when the steel company was paid, they would pay our client. In 2001 the law changed. A consignment was now treated just like a PMSI. We negotiated carefully with the steel company to get the proper documentation in place before they filed for bankruptcy under chapter 11. The steel company understood that it needed our client's cooperation once a bankruptcy was filed. With the proper documentation in place well in advance, our client got paid and kept a customer.

Defense Strategies
Beyond The Red Zone

Increase recoveries by getting help from skip tracers, asset locators, small claims courts, collection professionals and creditors' rights attorneys.

At the early stages, delinquent accounts are essentially an intramural sport. It's "our collection department" versus "our slow paying customers." If collections can't score after repeated attempts, it's time to change the game and the players. The new game is called "Recovery" and outsiders are substituted for the collection staff. The "Get P.A.I.D." goal remains, but creditors move the game to another field.

A. Assistance From the Outside

Why use outsiders? They provide a fresh voice, desirable incentives, new methods and a commitment to collect, if collection is possible. They give the customer and collection team a break from constant bickering, frustration and high pressure.

The best recovery professionals are motivated, aggressive, tactful and clever. They treat the debtor with respect and fairness. And they are firm with them, sometimes very firm.

Five interrelated specialties make up an effective recovery team:

- Skip tracers
- Asset locators
- Collection professionals
- Clerks of court
- Creditors' rights attorneys

1. Skip Tracers

Skip tracers make their living finding people who have moved without leaving a forwarding address. The person they are pursuing is the "skip." Some skips are hard-core and elusive — credit criminals who know how to hide. Others new to dodging creditors are "unintentional skips." They have simply neglected to leave a forwarding address and are more easily traced.

Public records and former neighbors are examples of tools of the trade for skip tracers. But the tracer's Swiss Army knife, the one tool that fits all, is the Social Security number. It's easy to see why. The Social Security Administration updates addresses every time someone applies for insurance, utilities, credit, a loan or an apartment rental. If a skip applies for any of these services in a new location, Social Security has the new address.

In Chapter 2, we recommended the inclusion of the owner's social security number on the credit application. Now is the time that information comes in handy.

It is not hard to find those who specialize in skip tracing. Searching the Internet will yield hundreds of agencies, large and small. But if your firm is a member of any of the country's major credit bureaus mentioned in Chapter 3, you need look no further. Armed with the owner's Social Security number and a "permissible purpose" as defined under the Fair Credit Reporting Act (FCRA), Dun & Bradstreet, National Association of Credit Management (NACM), Experian, TransUnion or Equifax can conduct a competent skip trace. Telephone numbers and Web sites for these bureaus are listed in Chapter 3. Also check with your collection agency or creditors' rights attorney.

The 1992 FCRA brought increased federal regulation to the nation's credit bureaus. Its goal was to insure accuracy and fairness in credit reporting. Privacy was added as a third goal by the 1999 Gramm-Leach-Bliley Act also known as the Financial Services Modernization Act.

There are five permissible purposes for a credit report in the FCRA's Section 604. The one for skip tracing also applies to extending credit: ". . . any consumer reporting agency may furnish a consumer report . . . to a person which it has reason to believe intends to use the information in connection with a credit transaction." Other legitimate and permissible purposes for a credit report include employment, eligibility for a license, business needs, child support, paternity suits and a court order. The law prohibits credit bureaus from helping a member fish for potential customers by entering a random number in the Social Security database. It also prohibits using a credit report as a subterfuge for obtaining other sensitive personal and financial information from consumers.

Credit reports have one down side: they are purely informative. The credit bureau may have found the skip's address, but they haven't contacted him, assessed his potential for recovery, found his assets or obtained payment. Professional skip tracers, especially those associated with collection agencies, law firms, banks and leasing companies, will take a few of these extra steps for an additional fee. But even with an expanded job description, skip tracers are not collectors.

That work is left to the collection agency or the creditors' rights lawyer. Skip tracers show their clients where the debtor can be found and, often, what he owns. Someone else opens the front door and goes inside. Skip tracers typically charge a flat rate for their services. Some have a "no find, no fee" policy.

2. Asset Locator

Closely related to the skip tracer is the asset locator. Does the missing debtor own a boat, automobile or airplane? Is there real estate in his or her name? Are there any large investments where the debtor owns more than 5% of a company's stock? What about open bank accounts or safe deposit boxes? For a fee, asset locators will conduct a nationwide search to find answers to these questions. Extra services include an assessment of the likelihood of recovery and a detailed valuation of the total assets found.

Reports from the skip tracer and asset locator are typically handed off to a collection agency or a creditors' rights attorney. In the previous chapter we discussed the services offered by each of these professionals and suggestions for choosing between them. Let's see what they do with the reports provided by skip tracers and locators and how they manage to collect when our intramural team could not.

3. Collection Professionals

Collection professionals move quickly to establish contact with debtors. Many call or visit debtors within 24 hours of starting a job. Being quick out of the chute does not mean they meet debtors unprepared. Crafty collectors come equipped with many well integrated and sharpened traits and abilities. These pros are part negotiator, guidance counselor, researcher and inventor. Their imagination and threshold for frustration reach skyscraper proportions.

The collection agencies that have been around a while use the old collection mantra, "Deal with me now or deal with an attorney later," with great subtly and finesse. Since many collection agencies have relationships with an attorney's office, this eventuality is believable, but it is also dangerous. It raises antagonisms as well as ingrained fears and resentments about being sued and countersuing. It gets the debtor in a win-lose, not win-win mind-set. For some slow payers with large indebtedness, avoiding litigation may be a good reason to pay or promise to pay. For many others, it is like waving a red flag in front of bull that will either dig in its heels or charge.

One alternative used by experienced collection professionals is a strongly worded letter from a creditors' rights attorney. The official looking letter on impressive stationery hints at litigation, but emphasizes resolution as a way of avoiding the courtroom. Timing is critical. Such a letter needs to come at the right time, from the right lawyer and say the right things. Longtime collection professionals are good at judging when and where to bring in the lawyers.

Negotiations and Other Tactics

Letters and the threat of litigation are not the only tools of a collection professional. They've learned that negotiating a clever, unexpected solution is what keeps frustrated creditors beating a path to their door. For example, collectors are experts at finding helpful people who assist in resolving an impasse. Many use the debtor's own banker, attorney or accountant to bring pressure on the debtor to pay up.

A collector tactic worthy of emulation is the short-term promise to pay. In Chapter 4, we recommended the collections staff wait 10 days after their first request for payment and another 10 days after their first demand letter. Collectors are beyond such leniency.

The best in the business insist on payment in two days, and they are in the debtor's face if that short deadline is missed. There are many ways to get a payment in the collector's hands that quickly. Overnight mail, "check by phone," credit cards and payment pick up are a few.

Collectors also look for non-monetary ways to settle a debt. If cash is short, some will barter with the debtor for equipment, property, deeds, supplies or a boat found by an asset locator. Such goods might come to more than the value of the claim itself. They may also trade liens on debtor's property for more time to pay.

Their role as the third party in a two-way battle also allows collectors the unique opportunity to soften polarized positions. Collectors may encourage an angry creditor to lift the credit hold they imposed on the debtor. This resumption of a business relationship would be in exchange for payment in full or at a collector-arranged discount. A good collector can also intervene to broker new business from a now-compensated creditor to a formerly errant debtor.

Innovative collectors discuss the possibility of exchanging part of the debt, say interest due or late fees, for the debtor's contribution to his or her favorite charity.

Giving that contested money to charity and not to the creditor may be all it takes to soften the debtor's resistance to paying the rest of the debt. Such an arrangement allows the debtor to save face, benefit a good cause, obtain a tax deduction and settle a debt.

Debtors, especially those with small balances, may need to be schooled in the effect of bad debt on their credit report and collectors make good teachers. Their lesson begins with a strong dose of reality: "Your company will still be in business if you refuse to pay my client's $600 bill, but what about the cost to your reputation if you are refused credit five years from now?" And the solution: "Pay now and my client will not have to inform the credit bureau of this bad debt."

Rates

Collection agencies typically provide their valuable services for 20% to 25% of the unpaid debt. The percentage can vary depending upon the size and age of the account. Be careful to check on other fees such as postage, listing charges and copying costs. Some creditors, possibly resentful of having to resort to a collection agency, work hard to negotiate a lower rate. We recommend working with the agency that has the best record of collection success in your industry and with your type of client. And we recommend paying a fair percentage. Those businesses that gain a reduction in the collector's rate may suffer an equal reduction in collector effort, enthusiasm and creativity. It is a good example of penny wise, dollar foolish.

Creditors who are resistant to placing the claim on a contingent fee are wise to remember what I said earlier about what retailers do when they have inventory that is out of season. They often discount it to get it moving. Similarly, vendors with delinquencies should consider discounting their receivables by placing them for collection on contingency.

4. Clerks of Courts

Using the Courts

The clerk at small claims court or the secretary at the magistrate's office play a minor but potentially valuable role in the recovery game. They provide the forms needed to file a complaint in small claims court. These government officials can also be counted on to provide useful information for first-time filers. The key role in small claims court is played by members of the collections team, not outsiders. In this fourth quarter play, the creditor's employees get back in the game.

No attorney is needed to file a complaint in many of the nation's small claims courts. Creditors can usually sue *pro se* (without legal representation). Sometimes, corporate (or LLC) creditors are required to have an attorney, since they are not natural persons. The entire procedure is effective and inexpensive, but creditors should know that small claims court is a trial, a fact discussed later when we look at the role of the attorney.

The beauty of the system is that the summons and complaint may be all that are needed to get paid by a previously defiant debtor. And the blank forms needed to start the process may be downloaded from the county government's Web site or obtained through the mail after a telephone inquiry.

It's been our experience that a good percentage of the debtors served with the summons pay up. When debtors ignore the summons or refer the matter to their attorney, creditors have a choice: continue to court themselves or retain an attorney to help them with the case. Attorneys are frequently involved in small claims when the jurisdiction is in a distant state. They can also be brought in at the last minute and may charge a minimum fee for representing the creditor at this early stage only.

Collecting on judgments

If the creditor wins in small claims court – and the success rate has been quoted as 90% or above - the court does not handle the logical next step: collection. One wise judge compared a judgment to a hunting license – successful creditors-now-plaintiffs are entitled to a "buck," but the court does not go out and shoot it for them. Collection options vary among the states. They include placing a "lien" against real estate or other assets and requesting periodic payments from the debtor-now-defendant. The sheriff plays a key role in collections in some states. He or she can seize assets and sell them ("sheriff's sale") or remove money from the defendant's cash register to cover the judgment ("till tap"). Plaintiffs request the sheriff's actions; they do not automatically follow a judgment.

The downside of this sensible "small claims" process is that claims are generally limited to about $5,000. Small claims court is not the place where creditors threatened by the dirty deeds of credit criminals find relief. But with inflation creep, states keep upping the definition of "small claim." Of the states checked recently, Georgia and Delaware had the highest limit, $15,000; Kentucky and Rhode Island the lowest at $1,500.

5. Creditors' Rights Attorney

Of all the outsiders playing in the recovery game, a creditors' rights attorney may be the only one who can act as player and coach. Attorneys are the "power forwards" who are involved in making the big plays and the coach who creates game-winning strategies. In their coach role, attorneys give advice and advocate for their players as well as represent and counsel them. In recent years, many have enlarged their team. Skip tracers, asset locators and trained collectors are on the bench with some collection lawyers.

One of the most valuable services a creditors' rights attorney brings to the playing field is advocacy. Good lawyers, like good bankers, are experienced friends who can speak for a creditor, stand up for their side and look out for their welfare. They advocate early in a business relationship by adding all the legalese (and protections) to a credit agreement. And they advocate in recovery in numerous ways including helping clients prepare for court. Even in small claims court, parties operate under the same rules as a civil trial. There are summons and complaints, and may be interrogatories, depositions, evidence, cross examinations and courtroom etiquette to understand and abide by.

For those who have never been inside a courtroom, it pays to have someone with you who knows the landscape and prevents you from getting lost.

Creditors' rights lawyers are also good at writing effective demand letters and sending them in a fear-inducing package. There is nothing quite so attention grabbing as an envelope with "Attorneys at Law" in the return address.

By this point in the debt recovery process, many creditors are tired of talking to their debtors. They have "had it up to here" and want someone else to intervene. But like all disputes from the playground to the office, face-to-face still trumps settlement by authority figures like principals, judges or bosses. After examining the case, a creditors' rights attorney might recommend alternative dispute resolution (ADR). Mediation and arbitration are conflict resolution tactics which can be useful for folks other than labor and management. To hold down expenses and help keep communication channels open between the creditor and debtor, some companies add ADR to their standard credit agreement.

B. Alternative Dispute Resolution

1. Mediation

Mediation and arbitration function quite differently.

In mediation, the parties work toward a non-binding, mutually agreeable solution with the mediator listening, offering suggestions and making recommendations. Attorneys are permitted in mediations, but when the mediator asks you to leave the room so she can discuss options and ideas with the other side, your attorney goes, too.

One of the *biggest mistakes* creditors make in mediation is to assume that somehow the mediator will know the debtor is lying. Data wins in research and preparation wins in all disputes from mediation to trial. Wise creditors let their attorney prepare and organize their case.

Mediators have a remarkably good track record: A very high percentage of commercial mediations are successfully resolved, many in short order.

2. Arbitration

Arbitration is like a trial but without the formality, rules of evidence and length. An arbitrator plays the role of judge, but with a twist: he or she is often experienced with disputes in the creditor's particular industry. Specialties include transportation, healthcare, energy, construction and disaster recovery. Witnesses testify and are cross-examined; exhibits, charts and records are presented and discussed. And the arbitrator listens and rules.

Ruling is the most important difference between mediation and arbitration. An arbitrator's decision is binding on the parties. That final authority does not come cheap: an arbitrator's hourly fee can run from $250 to $400. That's $1,500 to $2,400 for each six-hour day. The considerable cost of arbitration requires the parties to give the arbitrator power to streamline procedures and rulings that might otherwise consume much more time (and expense) in a court. Even large dollar disputes can bypass the courts and be resolved through arbitration. But, like mediation, preparation is the key to success. If your attorney can organize and guide the process for you, that experience may win the day.

The American Arbitration Association centralizes many of the rules that govern commercial arbitration. For more information about their role, visit their Web site: www.adr.org. The jury is still out on the questions of the effectiveness of ADR in debtor-creditor disputes. Since many disputes are raised because the debtor simply does not want to pay, it is often hard to get the debtor to agree to an ADR process. If the ADR agreement is in the original credit agreement, it may pass under the radar.

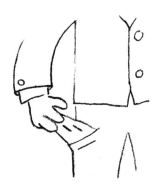

Some debtors are so lacking in money, income or property that they are virtually "judgment proof." Taking them to court just means spending more money to obtain nothing in return. A creditors' rights attorney can be employed to investigate a debtor's ability to pay. They check to see if assets are covered by liens or owned by a spouse or if there are pending judgments against the debtor.

Coupled with an asset search report, a creditors' rights attorney can guide clients toward the river where the chances of catching a big fish are the greatest. Judgment proof debtors represent a dry pond – a place where only trouble, not fish, resides.

C. Settlement Without Trial

There is a principle of psychology that says, "As a person gets closer to a goal with both positive and negative aspects, there is a tendency to avoid the goal."

Think of asking for a raise. You want the extra cash (+) but fear being told you don't deserve it (-). As you close in on the boss's door, you want to forget the whole idea. The goal in the case of debtor vs. creditor is not asking for a raise, but a trial. As the trial gets closer, the debtor's "urge to avoid" increases. A creditors' rights attorney capitalizes on that tendency by facilitating a settlement without a trial.

A number of arrangements are possible:

- The attorney negotiates installment payments with the debtor and postpones the trial until just after the last payment is expected. No payment? We go back to court.

- The attorney enters a consent judgment on the date set for trial with this statement: "Your honor my client and the defendant have reached a settlement."

The details are laid out for the judge and if the defendant agrees in front of the judge, the agreement carries the weight of a judge's ruling at trial.

- Closely resembling a consent judgment is placing the settlement on the record. Both parties appear before the judge and state that the case has been settled. Details are on the court record, but there is no judgment per se, just a written account of the terms of your agreement. If the debtor does not pay as agreed, your attorney must file an action to have the settlement enforced. Although more cumbersome than a consent judgment, this is a popular settlement option.

D. Trial as an Alternative

If all else fails, there is litigation, a costly, time-consuming, frustrating, but occasionally necessary way to resolve disputes. This is the process of filing suit in the proper court, navigating through the preliminary and pre-trial procedures, presenting convincing arguments at trial (if required) and receiving a judgment in the creditor's favor.

In the process, names change again: creditors become plaintiffs, debtors are renamed defendants. We are a long way from calling the parties "sellers" and "customers" and, for better or worse, a trial usually dooms the resumption of normal seller/customer relations.

Like settlements, preliminary and pre-trial procedures take us down many intriguing avenues for getting paid:

1. Summary judgment: If there are no facts in dispute, your attorney can file a motion for summary judgment. Some judges award a partial summary judgment – the defendant is liable for paying the debt, but actual damages are decided later.

2. Pre-Judgment Attachments: If your attorney can make the case that the defendant intends to destroy or dispose of property, some states allow the property to be attached or seized before judgement. This may be an effective System when defendants are relocating their business to Mexico or China. Combining attachment with other provisions in your credit agreement such as jurisdiction and choice of law provision (see chapter 2) makes pre-judgment attachment an attractive relief system. Remember that attachments are not judgments; they occur before judgments and are meant to maintain the status quo.

3. Injunctions: Defendants can be stopped from taking certain actions prejudicial or damaging to the plaintiff through injunctions. The most common situation is when the debtor is about to sell or liquidate a business or assets critical to the case. Injunctions temporarily or permanently halt the sale.

4. Post-Judgment: The final way a creditors' rights attorney helps in recovery is in the post-judgment phase of litigation, after the client has won the case and needs some muscle to collect on the judgment. As teens about to take the family car for a spin, we've heard the parental mantra: "Don't become a statistic." Our parents wanted us home safe, not in the hospital. After a trial, creditors don't want to become a judgment recovery statistic, but one in three "winners" is faced with an uncollectible judgment. Credit criminals can escape untouched even when they lose in court.

Failure to collect for one out of three clients is a challenge for the legal profession. But with dogged determination and personal attention, we can improve on a 33% success rate.

Here are a few of my favorite post-judgment success stories.

After obtaining a $7,000 judgment against a plumbing contractor, we sent the sheriff to the place of business to seize the debtor's equipment. The business was located out of town inside a fenced yard. No one was there when the deputies arrived so they left without taking anything.

A few days later one of our collectors came back from lunch and told me that the plumbing contractor's truck and compressor were on Grant Street blowing out the sprinkler lines for flower beds in the middle of the street.

I immediately headed for the sheriff's office which was at the same end of Grant Street as the contractor's truck. I was able to get a deputy to find the papers, take a walk outside and seize the truck and the compressor from the workers on the job. The contractor paid a couple of days later in order to redeem his equipment.

A number of years ago, we had a large judgment against two brothers who previously operated a gun store. We did the obvious thing and had the sheriff seize (or levy on) and sell their inventory. Their small inventory did not cover the judgment, so we served them with a subpoena to come to a deposition to testify about their assets. We held the deposition in the rural courthouse. During the deposition, one brother testified about the company truck that was parked outside. While the deposition continued, one of our staff members walked over to the sheriff's office and arranged for a deputy to go outside and tow the truck away.

As the deposition continued, we learned about their bank accounts in a local bank. We again walked to the sheriff's office and arranged for an attachment to be served on the bank. By the time the brother left the courthouse, the company bank accounts were attached and their truck was gone!

The Final Defense
Dealing With Bankruptcy

Don't take a back seat when debtors declare bankruptcy. Assert your rights and win.

Since 1788 when bankruptcy became part of Article 1 of the Constitution, Congress has tried to get bankruptcy law right. They've not had an easy time of it. Balancing the rights of creditors with the needs of debtors has not been easy.

In their defense, "balance" was not always in style. The bankruptcy laws Congress passed in the late 18th century began as legalized punishment. Debtors' prisons were not just a reality in Charles Dickens' David Copperfield. We had them here too for our first 50 years. When they were abolished on the federal level in 1833, Congress struggled to find better ways to reconcile creditors and debtors. Three laws concerning bankruptcy jurisdiction and business liquidation were passed by Congress before 1898. All were repealed.

With the Bankruptcy Act of 1898, Congress found the treasured middle way. This law not only created the equivalent of the modern bankruptcy judge who helped settle disputes — an aid to businesses — but it also loosened constraints on debtors. The Act developed broad categories of debtor-exempt assets as well as ways to rehabilitate debtors, not just liquidate their assets.

A. Overview of Bankruptcy

1. Bankruptcy Law from 1978 to the Present

These innovations survived for 80 years, until the Bankruptcy Reform Act of 1978 created 94 independent bankruptcy courts within the federal judiciary to oversee the process. It also made it easier for businesses and individuals to file bankruptcy and reorganize. The 1978 Reform Act, perhaps more than any other law, legitimized and popularized bankruptcies in the United States. It changed bankruptcy from a rare, headline-producing event to something more commonplace.

Legal practices across the country see the effects of the 1978 law everyday. The 1978 law has been amended several times - in 1984, 1986 and 1994. In 2005, after years of debate, President Bush signed the Bankruptcy Abuse Prevention and Consumer Protection Act (BAPCPA). Although many sections apply only to consumer debt and bankruptcy trustees, the newest bankruptcy law contains some powerful tools for limiting filings and defending creditors' rights.

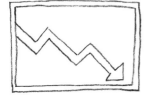

Bankruptcy filings spiked right before the October 17, 2005 effective date of BAPCPA, then dropped like a rock by more than 70% during 2006 as compared to 2005. This drop was attributable to the rush of filings in 2005 (to beat the change in the law) and the new limits in the law. However, 2007 saw steady increases in monthly filings. The numbers have not reached pre-October 2005 levels, but they seem to be climbing steadily.

2. The Purposes of Bankruptcy Law

Through the years, Congress has defined and refined the essential purposes of bankruptcy law. Three have emerged. Although some have more of a business flavor, all apply to business and personal bankruptcy.

• **Fresh start:** The bankruptcy code first attempts to give debtors a fresh start, to get individuals and businesses back on their feet as productive citizens. Applied to business, the intent is to keep a struggling company alive, not kill it. But creditor feeding frenzies do occur in bankruptcy and there is often no company left to start fresh.

• **Equitable distribution:** The law also seeks an equitable distribution of assets to the various creditors. That means establishing a system of creditor priority – determining which class of creditors is at the head – or the back - of the line.

• **Debtor rehabilitation:** Finally, the code institutionalizes a plan for reorganizing one's business or personal life. The goal here is debtor rehabilitation.

3. Specialties

In all aspects of the law, attorneys take sides. Some prosecute, others defend. Similar divisions occur in bankruptcy. Attorneys are generally either debtor's counsel or creditor's counsel. Since this book is written from a strong creditor's point of view, it should come as no surprise that our firm focuses on creditors' rights. That emphasis began more than 40 years ago under my father's leadership. Today our law firm has the largest team of board-certified creditors' rights specialists in Pennsylvania. In the past 10 years alone, we have handled more than 100,000 creditors' rights cases for clients.

Businesses or individuals that need help deciding how, when and where to file for bankruptcy, need a debtor's counsel. There are hundreds throughout the country including, at times, our firm. In special cases, we represent business debtors attempting to reorganize their businesses and equitably distribute assets.

B. Voluntary Bankruptcy

Most bankruptcies are voluntary.
Company officials file a petition with the bankruptcy court (a debtor's petition) usually in the state where its headquarters is located. Filing involves providing the court with schedules of assets and liabilities, current income and expenditures, statement of financial affairs, a schedule of contracts and other documents.

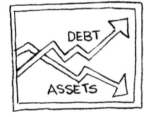

The true beginning of voluntary bankruptcy occurs long before papers are filed. A company is considered bankrupt or insolvent when, according to its own balance sheet, debts exceed the fair market value of assets. The law is careful to note that companies in trouble often try to reduce their assets both on and off the balance sheet. Fewer assets mean less that has to go to creditors in bankruptcy. So the law takes a hard look at assets – funds, goods, equipment, property, inventory – transferred before insolvency is discovered. To the consternation of many creditors, a customer's payment of its legitimate debts may be avoided (or undone) as a fraudulent or preferential transfer in bankruptcy court.

There is another way of determining insolvency, one that is more obvious to creditors: the debtor company stops paying its bills on time. This method is more straight forward and makes it easier to prove bankruptcy. Anyone who followed the Enron cover-up knows that balance sheets and other financial documents are open to a variety of interpretations.

C. Involuntary Bankruptcy

Under the code, three creditors with debts totaling at least $12,300 may file an involuntary bankruptcy petition (a creditor's petition). If there are fewer than 12 creditors, a single creditor with a claim of at least $12,300 may file the petition. All costs for prosecuting a successful creditor's petition are eventually borne by the debtor's bankruptcy estate. The key word here is "successful." Bankruptcy courts are not kind to creditor petitions made in bad faith. Wise creditors consult a creditors' rights attorney before filing involuntary bankruptcy on their own.

The term "estate" requires a bit of explanation, too. When bankruptcy proceedings have begun, an estate is created that is the temporary legal owner of all of the debtor's assets. Creditors are paid from the non-exempt assets of the estate.

1. Conditions for Involuntary Bankruptcy

When should creditors take action? There are a number of well accepted benchmarks.

- **Fraudulent transfers:** When an insolvent debtor transfers assets to anyone — relatives, general partners, directors, officers, managers or its affiliates — in order to have less to give to creditors, it's time to act. Transfers of assets for less than fair value may also be suspect. My father always said, "When in debt, you must be just before you can be generous." Such transfers may be fraudulent. Bankruptcy trustees, those federal officials who investigate the financial affairs of debtors, will query everyone, even legitimate creditors, trying to determine if they are part of a fraudulent transfer. Our advice: check with a creditors' rights attorney before returning any payments made by a customer in voluntary or involuntary bankruptcy. Remember that trustees are on fishing expeditions for fraudulent transfers, and they have to prove their assertions. Legitimate payments on debt may be fraudulent transfers, but there may also be defenses.

When a debtor sells assets at fire sale prices without considering creditors, take action. This scheme is one of the greatest concerns among creditors seeking help from our firm. Intent to defraud is one critical component here. Creditors suspect fraud when debtors sell assets at bargain basement prices or in the language of the court, "at less than reasonably equivalent value." Fraudulent conveyance is a variation of fraudulent transfer – instead of giving a creditor's equipment to Uncle Charlie, a debtor sells it to him for 10 cents on the dollar.

- **Preferential Transfers:** When a debtor is paying other creditors, but not you, it's time to act. These preferential transfers are often payoffs to the debtor's friends. They insure that after bankruptcy, the friends will continue to ship product to the debtor. Such transfers violate the equal distribution purpose of bankruptcy law and constitute a valid reason for involuntary bankruptcy. Bankruptcy courts have the power to negate preferential transfers and recover assets for equal distribution.

- **Delaying Tactics:** When a debtor repeatedly ignores requests for payment, it may be time to act. Delays may be the tip of a fraudulent or preferential transfer iceberg. In Chapter 5 we discussed the various reasons to step outside our 10-point collection plan and seek immediate help. In cases where creditors think that delays indicate insolvency, a creditors' rights attorney can investigate and may advise filing.

- **Active Secured Lenders:** Secured lenders are at the top of the payment priority list; unsecured lenders are at the back of the line. When unsecured lenders sense insolvency and then observe secured lenders acting aggressively to secure a company's assets, involuntary bankruptcy may be their best option. By petitioning a single forum and avoiding the hassle of various state courts, unsecured creditors may be able to gain an advantage on the debtor's assets. Something, as we always say, is better than nothing.

- **Debtor Autopsy:** Involuntary bankruptcy petitions can be useful in situations where a creditor simply doesn't know what happened to a customer that suddenly went "belly up." Rather than letting the company dissolve and disappear, creditors often find involuntary bankruptcy a useful tool in conducting an "autopsy" of the debtor's business. Little is generally gained financially from this endeavor, but it can be a useful lesson and a guide for amending collection policies.

2. Timing

Timing is critical in involuntary bankruptcy. The date a petition is filed determines how far back a trustee can look to avoid transfers. For preferential transfers, the "reach back" period is 90 days from the filing date. It is one year if the recipient of the transfer is an "insider" such as an officer or director. During that period the debtor is presumed to have been insolvent.

In regards to fraudulent transfers, "reach back" is even longer. It's two years from the filing date. That is one year longer than the pre-BAPCPA law. Bankruptcy courts are empowered to nullify fraudulent transfers made during that period and include them in the assets to be distributed among the creditors. This is important because savvy, asset-rich debtors often quietly form a new company during insolvency. The sole purpose of the new company is to receive assets from the insolvent one at less than market value. Without intervention, all that would be left for creditors to pick over is a worthless shell corporation with little or no assets.

D. Chapters of the Bankruptcy Code

Essentially there are only two kinds of American-style bankruptcies: liquidation and reorganization. The rules of bankruptcy are codified in Title 11 of the United States Code (USC). Within Title 11 are the now famous chapters that address specific bankruptcy issues.

Chapters 1 and 3 are mostly administrative with various definitions, duties, general provisions and penalties. Chapter 5 is required reading. It defines and discusses in detail creditors, debtors and the bankruptcy estate. Chapter 7 concerns estate liquidation. It defines what property is exempt and what must be sold to repay creditors. Chapter 9 provides protection for a financially distressed municipality and public agencies. Bankruptcy allows these entities time to formulate a plan for adjusting their debt. Chapter 11 details how a business can continue to operate while formulating plans to reorganize and repay its creditors. Chapter 12 focuses on only two occupations: farmers and fishermen with a regular income. Repayment options for bankrupt individuals with regular incomes are described in Chapter 13. Chapter 15 relates to interational or "cross border" insolvencies.

There are a few omissions. There are no Chapters 2, 4, 6, 8, 10 or 14.

The chapters that keep attorneys, accountants and bankruptcy trustees busy are 7, 11, 12 and 13. Based on the amount of newspaper ink and television news time devoted to the collapse of major corporations such as Enron, WorldCom and Global Crossing, you'd expect Chapter 11 to top the list. Instead, Chapter 11 comes in close to the bottom in terms of case frequency. In 2006, 5,163 companies filed for bankruptcy under Chapter 11. That is eight tenths of one percent of the total number of bankruptcies that year. The majority, 58% or 360,890 of the 617,660 cases in 2006 were filed under Chapter 7. Chapter 13 was second with 41% or 251,179 cases. The remaining fraction was handled under Chapter 12. Chapter 7 led the way in terms of decreased filings. From 2005 to 2006, there were 78% fewer Chapter 7 filings. Chapter 13 had 39% fewer and Chapter 11, 24%. Much of that decrease was short-lived and caused by filers beating the October 2005 law change.

E. Chapter 7 Bankruptcy

1. About Chapter 7

Liquidation bankruptcy is referred to as a "Chapter 7 Bankruptcy." More specifically, it's either a consumer Chapter 7 or a business Chapter 7 bankruptcy.

Debtors that file under Chapter 7 are automatically assigned the services of a trustee, usually an attorney or accountant. A trustee has many possible roles: liquidating and distributing assets, representing the creditors, reviewing the debtor's claims, filing objections, opposing the debtor's discharge if necessary, initiating litigation and operating the debtor's business. Trustees do not decide questions such as discharge; that is left to the judge. Generally, a trustee oversees the administration of the case. They are paid from the bankruptcy court filing fee and, in the rare case with assets to distribute, by a percentage of the assets they handle.

Immediately after filing, debtors receive one of the key benefits of balanced bankruptcy law: an automatic stay. This protection triggers an injunction against law suits, collection calls, repossessions and foreclosure sales. Creditors can obtain relief from an automatic stay, but they must show cause to the bankruptcy judge. Relief from stay is an area of specialty for our law firm. There will be more about relief from automatic stay later.

2. Discharge and Dismissal

Earlier we said that a trustee (or a creditor) can oppose the debtor's discharge. What is discharge? When debts are discharged they are no longer enforceable against the debtor. Discharge is a major goal of a debtor. One can oppose discharge for a variety of reasons. The ones that concern us are transferring, concealing or destroying assets, or financial records and obtaining credit by fraud. If the judge agrees, the case continues, but so do the debts.

Denial of discharge is not the same as denial of "dischargeability of a debt" and not the same as dismissal. In some cases, a debt is not dischargeable. This can result from how the debt was created or how the debtor treated the creditor during the case. Examples are certain tax or student loan debts, along with debts incurred through fraudulent financial statements.

Dismissal occurs when the case is ended prematurely. Such dismissal can be sought voluntarily or can be a punishment to prevent a misbehaving debtor from getting the benefits of the automatic stay and discharge.

Soon after filing, debtors must rather quickly provide the trustee with schedules (lists) of their assets, liabilities and vendors. They must also choose between their state's list of exempt assets and the list provided by the bankruptcy code. Generally, debtors may keep exempt assets such as retirement and profit sharing plans; such funds are usually not subject to liquidation.

3. The 341 Meeting

One of the trustee's first duties is to convene what has been called a "341 meeting." The name refers to the section of Chapter 3 that requires it. Creditors are invited to attend a 341 meeting, but few accept the invitation. The trustee presides; there is no judge at a 341 meeting. Since debtors must make at least one appearance during bankruptcy proceeding, they usually attend this meeting. Debtors that attend, testify under oath. The trustee's goal is to get all of the administrative t's crossed and i's dotted. They question, not interrogate, during this meeting:

"Are the schedules of assets and liabilities complete? Any corrections or changes?" Few 341 meetings last more than an hour.

4. Priorities

After the bankruptcy filing, the trustee takes control of the debtor's non-exempt assets, liquidates them, sometimes sells them at a public auction, pays the case's administrative expenses and distributes any remaining funds to the creditors. Distribution is made according to the priority order established by the bankruptcy code. In general, secured creditors are paid first. This class includes creditors with a security interest or lien on property or equipment purchased by the debtor. Secured claims are paid in full or until the proceeds from the asset sale are exhausted. If there is money left, it goes to the debtor's unsecured creditors. Unsecured creditors have certain statutorily-prescribed priority. Domestic support obligations, taxes and employee benefits are paid in full before general unsecured creditors. These lowest creditors get paid in equal shares (pro rata). Anything that is left goes to the debtor or to the shareholders or owners of the business.

5. Who files under Chapter 7?

In general, Chapter 7 attracts three kinds of distressed businesses. Either they don't have enough assets to operate or have too much debt to restructure or have no viable business concept.

6. Converting from one chapter to another

Bankruptcy, like a swift kick in the pants, helps clear the mind. As business owners envision their assets sold and their business shuttered, some realize they want their company to stay alive. Chapter 11 offers a variety of survival options for businesses with a chance of success, everything from extended repayments and debt reduction plans to comprehensive reorganization. The code allows debtors who see the light to petition the court for a conversion of their case to Chapter 11.

The court also allows petitions in the other direction – from Chapter 11 to 7. This is a smart move for companies with little left to reorganize. It may also be a decision forced on debtors by the court if it finds their Chapter 11 plans vague, impossible, in bad faith or if the debtor defaults. Conversion may also be requested by a committee of

unsecured creditors who think a debtor's plan for turning the business around is unworkable or inadequate. Sometimes the creditors think they are better off with the business dead than alive.

F. Chapter 11

1. About Chapter 11 Bankruptcy

Chapter 11 represents the second form of American style bankruptcy– the business reorganization. This process focuses on the second and third purposes of bankruptcy – equitable distribution of assets and debtor rehabilitation.

Negotiations are central to Chapter 11. When debtors and creditors "give and take," viable and successful plans result. Our law firm recommends strong creditor input. We have learned that while many initial reorganization plans are devised by the debtor, the process works best when both debtor and creditor fully and actively participate in plan development. The last study I saw said there was almost no likelihood of payment to creditors unless there was a committee of unsecured creditors formed. And even then it was only about 10% of the cases paid anything to creditors.

2. Differences Between Chapter 7 and 11

There are a few significant differences between Chapters 11 and 7:

- Debtors remain in possession of their property, can borrow funds, and conduct business during Chapter 11 proceedings. In general, debtors have all the rights of trustees in Chapter 7. For many decisions that would be considered in the normal course of business, debtors do not need court approval. They assume a new title, however: Debtors in Possession and yes, that is abbreviated, DIP.

- In Chapter 11, trustees are optional and are only appointed for cause, in cases where benefits outweigh costs or at the request of creditors. Creditors often request a trustee when a reorganization case is stagnating and when a savvy, experienced trustee replacing current management, would move the case toward reorganization. Trustees are also a viable option for creditors when other options such as relief from stay, conversion and dismissal are unavailable.

Trustees are rare, but when appointed, are generally helpful to creditors.

They usually come in when there is fraud or mismanagement and when the company needs to be run in a straightforward manner, or liquidated expeditiously. Trustees add an extra sense of fairness to the Chapter 11 process.

- The U.S. Trustee appoints a committee of unsecured creditors to consult, research, investigate and participate in the entire plan-forming process. When a creditor committee receives competent and experienced legal and financial counsel, it is more aggressive. In our experience, aggressiveness usually translates into a better plan from the debtor – one that maximizes positive cash flow and benefit to the creditors. The typical committee consists of three to seven members selected to represent the class of unsecured creditors. They may hire attorneys and accountants to advise them; these professional fees are paid by the bankruptcy estate. The Trustee may appoint more than one committee. In some cases, there have been separate committees appointed to represent the interest of stockholders and employees.

3. Chapter 11 Plan Process

The Chapter 11 Plan Process typically
involves seven fairly distinct steps. At each
step, creditors have exploitable advantages.

- **Exclusivity Period:** After filing, the DIP
  has 120 days to develop and file a plan
  of reorganization. Although negotiations
  are key to Chapter 11 (and a specific
  right of the Committee), debtors usually
  attempt to develop their first plans within
  their own corps of officers and advisors
  and in isolation from creditors. The court
  usually grants extensions if requested.
  After expiration of the exclusivity period,
  the committee of creditors or any other
  party-of-interest can propose a plan. We
  recommend that the creditor committee
  utilize this time to analyze the debtor's
  business and formulate reorganization
  strategies of their own.

- **More Acceptance:** The DIP has 60
  days to obtain acceptance of the plan
  from the creditors. This is the time when
  creditor home work pays off. With help
  from their accountants, the committee
  should determine the liquidation value

of the debtor company. This is a vital statistic if ever there was one.

If the debtor's plan yields less than what would be achieved through liquidation, creditors may lean toward converting to Chapter 7 and causing liquidation. They opt for a "Better dead than alive" resolution.

During these negotiations, creditors must be assured that the debtor's plan includes ways of increasing revenue, cutting costs, downsizing and liquidating supplies and other assets. They must insist on a clear timetable for accomplishing each business-saving action and on a backup plan if these strategies fail.

In some cases, we recommend that the creditors formulate a plan of their own, a tactic endorsed by the bankruptcy code. Creditor plans often call for canceling all existing stock, issuing new stock, and creditors serving as the new company's board of directors. Safe to say that few debtors include these creditor-friendly features in their plans.

- **Disclosure Statement:** Any plan proponent must develop and file a disclosure statement with the court. A disclosure statement is similar to a prospectus and just as thorough. It contains detailed financial and qualitative information that would help investors make an intelligent and informed decision about the plan and the company. The court expects to see a liquidation analysis as well as a discussion of the anticipated future of the company. When creditors insist that the debtor's plan meets all of the court's expectations as outlined in Section 1123, they leave Chapter 11 with a stronger plan and one with a better than average chance of turning around a disabled business.

- **Review:** The court conducts a hearing to determine if the disclosure statement contains "adequate information." If not, the debtor is ordinarily given an opportunity to amend. Once the disclosure statement is found to contain adequate information, it and the plan are distributed to the creditors for a vote.

- **Voting on the Plan:** Only members of impaired classes are entitled to vote on the plan. Unimpaired classes – those classes whose rights are not modified by the plan, are not entitled to vote. Voting is by class and there may be many classes in one case. A class accepts a plan when at least two-thirds in dollar amount and more than one-half in number **voting** approve the plan. When the creditor committee feels strongly about the plan, for or against, it is important for the committee to advise members of its class to vote.

- **Court Confirmation:** The court has the final say. It confirms, does not confirm, dismisses or converts the case. While this step may seem to be completely in the hands of the court, don't be fooled. The decision to confirm can become a legal battleground. Competent and experienced legal and financial guidance are essential at this step.

  In general, the court confirms a feasible, good faith plan when it is fair and equitable (that is, it distributes assets so that classes receive at least as much as a chapter 7 liquidation) and all impaired classes have voted in favor of the plan.

The last provision causes some haggling. All impaired classes may not vote in favor of the plan. This forces the court to make a special provision to override its own rules. This is known as the "cram down" as in "cram down one's throat." The court crams down the plan when at least one impaired class has accepted it, it is fair and equitable and it distributes assets according to a court-agreed priority. The best protection here for creditors is that this also requires reference to the "absolute priority rule." In essence, if the unsecured creditor class rejects the plan, it cannot be "crammed down" unless (a) the unsecured are being paid in full and (b) no junior class (usually owners) keep or receive anything on account of their pre-bankruptcy ownership.

- **Implementation:** Confirmation is hardly the end of the bankruptcy process. Creditors committees that have negotiated well make sure that provisions are made for periodic monitoring of the debtor's compliance with the plan. They have also insured that they are treated like members of the board and receive periodic financial statements.

They have also inserted provisions for the acceleration of debt in the event of default. The possibility of default is a central theme among well coached creditors committees. They make sure that they have the right to sue in state court in case the debtor defaults.

4. Other Creditors' Rights

Our law firm argues for creditors' rights throughout the entire Chapter 11 plan negotiation process. A number of them have been touched on already, but there are still others.

• Adequate protection and relief from stay are related and are best understood with an example. Assume that salesperson Mary Smith sold ABC Company $1,000 worth of merchandise on credit and secured a lien on the property worth $800. Bill Turner also sold ABC Company $1,000 in goods on credit, but secured the transaction with a lien on property worth $1,500. ABC filed for bankruptcy under Chapter 11 and received an automatic stay that prevented Smith and Turner, both secured creditors, from foreclosing on the property.

Because Turner's lien is for more than the value of the property, he is defined as an oversecured creditor. He can petition the court for adequate protection usually in the form of interest payments by ABC on his claim of $1,000 as well as the attorney's fees and other damages.

Smith is "under water." She generally gets limited adequate protection because there is a $200 deficiency between her claim ($1,000) and the lien ($800). The court would not reasonably allow the Company to pay interest on a $1,000 claim when a lien on the property is for a lesser amount. So what's Smith to do? She is an undersecured creditor, with a $200 deficiency or she is unsecured for $200 and secured for $800. That will make a difference at plan time.

What we might do in Smith's case is to argue that she needs the stay lifted because the property, now being held by DIP, is losing value and may decline to below even $800 the lien amount. If Smith is allowed to foreclose – and that would require the court to lift the automatic stay — she may be able to sell the merchandise for something close to the lien amount.

• BAPCPA, the new 2005 Bankruptcy Law change, provided vendors with still another tool for collecting debt in bankruptcy court. Under Section 503(b)(9), creditors are granted an administrative priority claim for the value of goods delivered to a customer within 20 days before the bankruptcy filing. Although the only deadline for filing a claim under Section 503(b)(9) is the time when creditors vote on the plan, we recommend sooner rather than later. An administrative priority claim raises the importance of the claim. It must be paid by the DIP before the plan is approved. For the court to confirm a plan all administrative claims must be paid in full.

• To take advantage of the right of reclamation requires quick creditor action. Generally, if creditors act within 20 days after bankruptcy was filed, they can reclaim goods delivered 45 days before the bankruptcy. But proper notice of reclamation must occur within that 20 day window or the right is lost. Reclamation specifically applies to the common situation where goods were sold on credit and delivered, but the invoices have not yet been paid.

G. Reorganization Without Bankruptcy

Plans of reorganization are central to a Chapter 11 bankruptcy. So what's to prevent a struggling company from devising a plan outside the harsh light of a bankruptcy court? Nothing. Those situations are called "workouts" or "creditor compositions." If the debtor and creditors resort to bankruptcy court to implement an already agreed plan, this is often called prepackaged bankruptcy or "prepacks."

A workout begins with a thorough analysis of the debtor's business by the company's accounting professionals. What are the liquidation and fair market values of the company assets? Liquidation, even outside of Chapter 7, is typically valued at 10% of retail value (fire sale prices). What debts and potential debts do we have? Are there written personal guarantees that must be satisfied? What are the realistic prospects for the firm?

Analysis is followed by a business plan tempered with the realization that creditors can force the company into bankruptcy. Part of any smart workout includes bringing creditors into the planning process, perhaps a representative committee with its own attorney and accountant.

Workouts often do work out. We once represented a group of creditors of a distressed coal company. As we were preparing to file suit, the company met with its accountants and developed a reorganization plan that they proposed to us and the other creditors. The result: a modified plan that was eventually accepted by the creditors and the debtor company. There was no bankruptcy court, but we loaded the plan with Chapter 11 protections just in case we had to go to bankruptcy court.

If we had to take the workout to bankruptcy court the plan must be confirmed by the court through a streamlined process. Prepackaged bankruptcy is most often used when enough creditors agree on the plan, but there are some that don't. The court can bind dissenting creditors through the voting rules described in Step 3 above.

H. On Learning from the Past

Over the years we have observed a few of the bankruptcy errors made by well meaning creditors. At the risk of sounding like a father with one last chance to give advice to a teen heading off to college, here are some precautions we recommend to all creditors facing or trying to out maneuver bankrupt customers.

- **The early bird catches the worm.** When a customer files for bankruptcy, act immediately. Find or call competent and experienced legal and financial counsel. Those critical 20, 45, 60 or 90 days slip by all too quickly.
- **An ounce of prevention is worth a pound of cure.** Review all of your sales contracts and agreements annually. For example, make sure that your sales and credit contracts supersede the terms and conditions on your customer's purchase orders.
- **Honesty is the best policy.** That holds true in all areas of life including bankruptcy court. Falsified records such as fraudulent accounting records and sales documents can land debtors and creditors in prison.

Conclusion

chapter 8

As is clear in the preceding chapters, credit policy has many dimensions. At the most obvious level, it is the way you get compensated for the work you do. But, as we've seen in the preceding pages, it is also a business strategy that can impact your relationships with customers, cash flow, profitability and growth potential.

In the first chapter, we framed a common conflict within many companies between the sales and credit functions. Sales departments typically like easy credit because it is thought to enhance customer relationships. Credit departments are typically 'enforcers,' believing that easy credit is akin to customer anarchy. What we've come to understand is that credit policy and marketing/sales strategy can go hand-in hand.

A. Balancing Sales and Credit Policy

1. The Role of the Invoice

Credit is part of the customer/client relationship. When you send an invoice to a customer, it is easy to assume that you are only documenting what the customer owes you. This is certainly true and necessary. But, many delays in payment are due to questions that arise about invoices. These questions are often not about the actual amount owed, but what these amounts are for.

It is amazing to see some invoices that raise questions simply by virtue of how little information is contained in them. For example, we once saw an invoice from a lawyer that had only one line item: "Legal Services," followed by an amount: $240,330. No time sheet. No task breakdown. Just "here's what you owe us."

There is no doubt that the law firm in question had done a lot work, and the amount was probably justified. But, such a document is not likely to go unquestioned or to make the client feel as though they received value for these services. Alternatively, invoices that clearly represent the services, products and value received can facilitate prompt payment, goodwill and in many respects, be seen as part of ongoing customer relationship management. In a best case scenario, the invoice, itself can be an extension of the marketing process, rather than an impediment to it.

Seen another way, the invoice can serve a number of other purposes:

• Documentation of the services. Clearly outlining or detailing what a customer has received reduces anxiety and questions related to an invoiced amount.

- Enhancing the Relationship. Invoices can be a good place to say 'thank you' for the business., listing "no charge" items and online payment.
- Represent the Benefits of Early Payment. Invoices can contain information related to discounts or bonuses (accumulated loyalty points) for early payment.
- Reminder of Understandings. Invoices can incentive early payment through clear descriptions of possible penalties for late payment. For example, a statement such as: Pay by June 5: $5,000/By July 5: $5,100, can reinforce credit policies already agreed upon.

2. The Psychology of Satisfaction

Apart from the information on the invoice that can represent value, easy credit, itself may not be the best strategy for maximizing customer loyalty. The reason has to do with the psychology of customer satisfaction.

Although it may be true that customers 'prefer' easy credit, the real issue is not whether they like your credit terms, but the value they assign to your product or service. A closer look at the concept of customer value reveals an interesting conundrum.

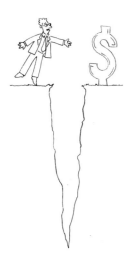

Customer satisfaction with a vendor or service provider depends on the perception of value they perceive. When easy credit is used as a marketing strategy to create value, a not-so-obvious problem occurs: perceived value can actually decline.

Perceived value is not a static concept. The value that people experience from a product or service changes over time. The reasons are complex, but, considerable research has confirmed that the highest level of satisfaction occurs closest to the time of receiving something. Although there are exceptions to this rule, in general, the longer the time of use, the lower the value is assigned to it.

This isn't good when it comes to credit or sales. Marketing and sales people want their customers to experience a high level of value. But when value declines over time, margins aren't the only thing that suffers.

A Payment Gap can actually cause the perceived value of the goods or services to decline. Related and even more interesting is the effect of payment on customer satisfaction.

As strange as it may seem, most people actually become 'invested' in a product or service only after they've paid for it. Real 'loyalty' actually begins only after you own something, not when you've received it. One of the most important sales techniques for some products and services is the 'advance' payment. The advance has two important effects. First, the seller gets paid before delivery. That's good for the seller and the bottom line. But, more interesting, is the effect on the buyer. Research confirms that the level of commitment actually increases once an advance has been made. Commitment through payment, in this sense, can actually enhance satisfaction and loyalty, rather than decrease it.

The implications for credit policy is clear. The longer the Payment Gap the lower the perceived value. That's the primary reason it's harder to collect the longer the Payment Gap.

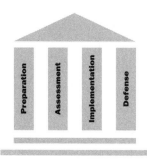

B. The Get P.A.I.D. System

1. The 4 Pillars of Credit Management

Understanding the costs of easy credit and benefits of a disciplined credit policy is only half the battle. As the preceding chapters have outlined, a well conceived credit policy that enhances customer relationship rests on four "pillars" of credit management: Preparation, Assessment, Implementation and Defense. Although inter-related, each phase serves a separate and critical role in ensuring that customer/clients understand and observe your credit policies. Together, these pillars help facilitate relationships based on parity between the buyer and seller, reduce cost and increase the potential that credit policy can become integrated with an organization's strategy for growth and profitability.

- Preparation provides the infrastructure for a sound credit policy by anticipating the possible contingencies that a company might face related to credit, and the formulating the tools needed to deal with them. Establishing the 'toolbox' provide guidelines and policies that address these possibilities.

- Assessment of credit risk is the process by which customers are qualified for credit. We've described the 3 "C's" of

credit (character, capacity and capital) and how to assess each customer according to these criteria. In addition, based on these assessments, we've outlined a variety of methods to mitigate risks, including credit limits, discounts and late fees.

- Implementation. We've emphasized the importance of time in collection, avoiding the expanding Payment Gaps and particularly, the Red Zone, when collection becomes difficult and expensive. Effective implementation depends on the "calendar of collection events" that helps you manage collections in a direct, standardized and efficient manner.

- Defense. When you reach the Red Zone, it's time for more aggressive measures to defend your policies. Here, a variety of experts can help.

2. Rationale for the Get P.A.I.D. System

A responsible and disciplined credit policy achieves two important goals: getting compensated for what you do and enhancing the relationship with your customers/clients, both important. These are the benefits. But, a more compelling reason to integrate the Get P.A.I.D. System underscores the importance of these principles: the cost of not observing them. Implied in the benefits of a well managed credit policy is a strong cautionary imperative: the hard cost s of easy credit, including finance cost, opportunity cost, collection cost, relationship cost and marketing cost. Easy credit can undermine all the important goals of a business, burdening it with:

- Loss of Revenue. Revenue is a time based exercise. Receivables aren't revenue. A product or service isn't technically sold until it's paid for.
- Loss of Profit. When collection costs are incurred, profit declines. As the charts on the previous pages represent, the cost of collection increases dramatically for each month a receivable remains uncollected. By the time you clocked 120 days, you've spent 40% of your potential revenue just to collect it. Not fun.
- Loss of Goodwill. Goodwill from providing easy credit becomes quickly eroded as soon as you start getting aggressive. There's nothing like penalty charges, collection letters and lawyers for building the kind of relationship that often ends in no relationship at all.

- Loss of Capital. If you're a bank, loaning money can be a good business. But, you're not a bank. And when you need capital from a real bank, slow paying customers don't help.

- Loss of Perceived Value. The longer the payment gap, the lower the perceived value of whatever you're selling.

C. Getting it Together

No system is bullet-proof. But, when you know what's coming, through Preparation, you've qualified through Assessment, Implemented you policy according to the calendar of collection and know the Defensive measures that work, at least you're ready. Ready for what? The Get P.A.I.D. System enables you to use credit policy as a business strategy to:

1 Improve your top line with more revenue

2 Improve your bottom line with more profit.

3 Improve your relationships with customers with greater loyalty

4 Improve your balance sheet by improving valuation

5 Improve your peace of mind with Preparation, Assessment, Implementation and Defense.

It's a system that's worked and a system that can work for you. To get paid, you need to Get P.A.I.D.

For a series of forms and guidelines that can help you implement the Get P.A.I.D. System for your company, go to our website: **www.getpaidsystem.com** for everything you need.

We conclude with a story:

It's forty below zero one winter night in Alaska. Pat is drinking at his local saloon and the bartender says to him, "You owe me quite a bit on your tab."

"Sorry," says Pat, "I'm flat broke this week."

"That's okay," says the bartender. "I'll just write your name and the amount you owe me right here on the wall."

"But," says Pat, "I don't want any of my friends to see that."

"They won't," says the bartender. "I'll just hang your parka over it until it's paid."

The bartender got P.A.I.D.